DA

The Strange Case of Franklin Jones

अर्दा

Also available from the MSAC Philosophy Group

Spooky Physics

Darwin's DNA

The Magic of Consciousness

The Gnostic Mystery

When Scholars Study the Sacred

Mystics of India

The Unknowing Sage

String Theory

In Search of the Perfect Coke

Is the Universe an App?

Adventures in Science

You are Probability

The Mystical

Digital Philosophy

The Sikhs

DA

The Strange Case of Franklin Jones

अदा

SCOTT LOWE AND DAVID LANE

Mt. San Antonio College
Walnut, California

Second Edition: June 2015

ISBN: 978-1-56543-300-7

MSAC Philosophy Group
Mt. San Antonio College
1100 Walnut, California 91789 USA

Website: http://www.neuralsurfer.com

Imprint: *The Runnebohm Library Series.*

Publication History: This book was first published in 1995 and contains original essays by Professor Scott Lowe and Professor David Lane.

Contents

The Paradox of Da Free John

Prefatory Note | May 2015

It has been 30 years since this essay was first published in the journal *Understanding Cults and Spiritual Movements*. I wrote my analysis of Da Free John shortly after my house had been robbed and ransacked by John-Roger Hinkins, founder and spiritual director of MSIA, in retaliation to a critical expose' I had penned about him in the very first issue of UCSM. John-Roger had also threatened to kill my wife and several of my informants through a worldwide smear campaign he had orchestrated from a front organization he created entitled *The Coalition for Civil and Spiritual Freedom* based (not surprisingly) out of a P.O. box he had (not very smartly) registered under his own name in Santa Monica, California.

Therefore, I was not too eager to have a nasty episode with another cult leader, so I decided that I would take a more distanced and academic approach when writing about Da Free John (now known more widely as Adi Da), who was then reaching the zenith of his fame. Yet, even then, I suspected that Da was hiding much about his private life and interactions with his inner circle. Ironically, just days after my long essay on Da was published, a disaffected woman devotee, who alleged that her guru had systematically abused her and others in his fold, filed a lawsuit against him and his group. It generated a media flurry since reports surfaced that Da had several wives and had indulged in all sorts of demeaning and damaging behavior.

I had been in regular contact for months prior to publication with Georg Feuerstein who, given his academic reputation in yoga circles, was serving as an intellectual spokesperson for Adi Da at that time. While Feuerstein was very responsive in providing feedback to various points of contention in my essay, he was disingenuous when discussing Adi Da's drug and sexual experimentation. Later, Feuerstein broke with Adi Da and wrote a book called *Holy Madness*, criticizing his former teacher. Frankly, I felt Georg Feuerstein should have been much more upfront earlier on, given that his confessional book tends to obviate his own responsibility in legitimizing Da's manifold transgressions.

As I mention in the postscript to this essay (which was incorporated in the 1994 book, *Exposing Cults: When the Skeptical Mind Confronts the Mystical*), I think I was much too easy on Adi Da and his undiluted narcissism. Yes, Da could on occasion write and say some very insightful, even brilliant, things, but much too often he was spouting off complete nonsense which only magnified (at least to me and other skeptics) his tireless megalomania.

Although I didn't mention him by name, the real target for my essay was Ken Wilber since I felt he had succumbed to a fundamental delusion in his hyperbolic praise of Da Free John by conflating an underlying spiritual message with the medium in which it was housed. Simply put, Wilber was wrong to think that Da was the supreme avatar of his time simply because he wrote some brilliant essays and gave thoughtful off the cuff satsangs. Writing wise notes doesn't make one wise, even if we may believe (watch the pun) otherwise.

Wilber did himself no favors (either to his reputation or to his intellectual integrity) by fawning so exaggeratedly over Da's mastership and penmanship, particularly when he criticized his readers for not following his praising of all things "Da." Ken Wilber's track record in endorsing so-called spiritual masters is so bad that one would be well advised to avoid any guru he recommends. The very fact that Ken Wilber could, after his fiasco with Adi Da, promote Andrew Cohen speaks volumes about his "integral" philosophy and its alleged merits for progressive thinking.

Reflecting back on Adi Da's life and work (he died unexpectedly of a heart attack in 2008 at his Fiji compound), I am convinced that Scott Lowe diagnosed his former teacher perfectly as suffering from the very narcissism he claimed engulfed his followers. Indeed, it may well be that much of Da's deep psychological insight into the human condition didn't stem from his self-proclaimed "enlightenment" but from observing day to day his own neurotic behavior and his own self-centered interactions with those closest to him. In any case, knowing what we do now about his uncouth antics, I would have definitely written a more critical piece on him today than I did thirty years ago. So with that caveat emptor read the following with a discriminating eye.

Distinguishing the Message from the Medium

There are very few spiritual teachers in the 20th century who could be termed religious geniuses. Da Free John is one of them. Since the beginning of his formal ministry in 1972 in southern California, Da Free John has produced a body of work that is unparalleled amongst new religious thinkers for its radical insight, comparative depth, and force of expression. He has won wide critical acclaim for his writings, eliciting praises from sociologists, psychologists, and theologians.

However, though Da Free John's writings have deservedly merited respect, the person himself remains a paradox. To many readers, the guru image he portrays juxtaposes with the impact of his message. Though Da Free John repeatedly stresses the need for transcending self-centeredness, he projects an egotistical air. Hence, while many individuals are deeply attracted to the philosophy of Da Free John, they are not drawn to the man. This, naturally, has led to a predicament in some seekers' minds on how to properly assess Da Free John and his teachings.

How does one distinguish a profound and viable spiritual message from the human medium that transmits it? This article, which is a generally positive overview of Da Free John's writings, is a response to that important question.

Confusing the Message with the Medium

In religious circles there is a tendency to confuse the message with the medium (and vice versa). If, for instance, an author writes convincingly, elegantly and profoundly about spiritual realization, the reader assumes that the writer must also be an enlightened being by virtue of his presentation. But, this is not always the case. Simply because one communicates ultimate truths well does not mean by extension that he is an embodiment of that highest realization. Indeed, the person may be quite the opposite.

A good example behind this fallacious equation of "the medium is the message" is found in the life and work of Alan Watts, the renowned philosopher of Zen Buddhism. Due to Watts' brilliant articulation of the perennial philosophy, some of his readers felt that he was a genuine Zen master, one who had transcended the ego and its limitations. However, as those close to Watts can attest, he was not an enlightened guru, nor did he pretend to be. Watts, like the rest of us, suffered from a number of human frailties, including alcoholism and womanizing. Though Watts wrote exquisitely about Nirvana, his writings do not entirely reflect his own samsaric condition.[1]

Personally, I have found this type of equative thinking among many of the followers in the new religious movements I have studied. Whereas the student may only be attracted to a particular element in the teachings, and not initially to the guru or the organization, he buys into the latter because he thinks they are inseparable. In other words, the would-be disciple presumes that he can't get "it" without all the accompanying paraphernalia.[2]

Take M.S.I.A. as a classic object lesson. What attracts most people to M.S.I.A. is the intriguing possibility of soul travel, not its lineage of "Mystical Travelers."[3] Yet, instead of selecting that kernel of the teaching, the neophyte swallows the whole philosophy believing that it is an all or nothing proposition.

Thus, following this contagious logic, the student accepts John-Roger Hinkins, the founder of M.S.I.A., as a genuine master solely by weight of his detailed account of the inner planes, since he has already accepted the validity of soul travel and tends to idolize the testimony of others who claim to be proficient at it. But, how is the unsuspecting seeker to know that John-Roger copied some of his material from other Eastern and New Age groups? Furthermore, how is he to realize that John-Roger's encounters with radiant beings--the hierarchy of inner masters--on the higher regions are literary fictions that he borrowed from another American offshoot of Ruhani Satsang? Fubbi Quantz, Rebazar Tarzs, and Jagat Ho do not exist, neither on this planet nor on "Tuza."[4]

The devotee ends up duped, and in the process of uncovering his naiveté he discards everything in the M.S.I.A. package (just like he bought it all in the beginning), even the one thing that was (and is) valid: out-of-body experiences.

Fundamentally, the mistake inherent in this kind of approach is that it lacks a consistent discriminating edge. One need not accept everything a spiritual movement offers because it has a single gleam of authenticity. Nor, on the other hand, one doesn't have to dismiss the benefit of a sincere guru because he is functionally illiterate or a "naive bumpkin."[5]

To illustrate this point even further (and I feel it is a crucial one for anybody involved in spirituality), think of Christianity. Now on the whole it is generally agreed that the Christian faith in its essential principles, as laid down by Jesus Christ, is a beneficial religion: moral, loving, self-sacrificing. However, this does not mean that we cannot make qualitative judgments on various parts of its organization and history. In fact, we do it all the time: Witness our criticisms of the Spanish Inquisition, the futility of the Crusades, the horrendous treatment of the Indians by the Missions of California, and so on.

We make a series of appraisements on Christianity, often criticizing a number of hypocrisies that have occurred throughout the ages. It is not until we think of Christianity in its highest ideals and occasional heroic examples (Mother Teresa, etc.) that we label the religion as "great," "beautiful," "transcendent." Comparatively, this is exactly what we should do with all spiritual teachers and groups but for the most part don't. Instead of retaining a critical perspective throughout our quest we prematurely abdicate our discriminating minds and often judge situations in an "either/or" manner. I have seen this many times in devoted disciples of north Indian gurus. One day the student says his master is "God incarnated," and on another he even doubts if his teacher is a decent human being.[6] The disciple oscillates between absolute verdicts, never realizing that his observations are but partial reflections of his own evolutionary growth.[7]

This now leads us to the main topic of this chapter: Da Free John. A number of individuals have rejected Da Free John's sweeping and dynamic message on the grounds that he is just another cult leader out to gain followers, fame, and wealth.[8] Moreover, some readers just cannot countenance Da Free John's "Crazy Adept" image. Across the years I have heard reactions that vary from: "He walks around half naked most of the time, wearing skimpy underwear." "I dislike his writing style; it's self aggrandizing." "Why does he keep changing the name of his organization?." "He is a poser, the epitome of the guru hype of the late 1960's. . . long hair, beard, walking staff, necklaces, then he shaves it all and goes for the egghead look. . . I don't buy it." "He has a hat/cap fetish." "Doesn't he drink his own urine?"[9]

Nevertheless, these same critics who disapprove of Da Free John's demeanor also reject his writings in their entirety since a "cult leader cannot possibly have any true or substantial insights on the nature of reality."[10] This, I believe, is a tragic mistake. The underlying spiritual message and the transmitting medium that conveys it, though related, are two distinct entities. To confuse the two betrays the fact that a corrupt religious group can present genuine teachings, or, that an authentic spiritual discourse can have an illegitimate expression.

I remember an incident in the spring of 1984 at the school where I was teaching which typifies this issue. I suggested to one of my brightest students that he read Da Free John's *The Paradox of Instruction* in order to get a better grasp of the varying yoga systems and their desired aims. The student took up my suggestion and casually mentioned the author and the book to his political science teacher, who, without a moment's reflection, called Da Free John "pop," implying that the guru had nothing really good to offer. When I heard of my colleague's reaction I asked the student to query his teacher further and find out if he had ever seriously read Da Free John's books. The answer, surprisingly, was no.[11]

Obviously, my colleague didn't appreciate Da Free John's guru portrayal, at least as it was depicted on the cover of his books. Yet, instead of stopping there and making a judgment call on Da Free John's pictures, my teacher associate carried his opinion even further and applied it to his writings as well--though he himself had never studied them. The sad part about this sort of prejudice is that it reinforces the very thing that teachers of all backgrounds (including those from secondary schools) argue against: "Don't judge a book by its cover." "Let the facts speak for themselves." Etc.

Quite simply, regardless of how we may view his "Crazy Adept" image, Da Free John is one of the best writers on the perennial wisdom (non-dualist philosophy) in North America. As Donald Evans, Professor of Philosophy at the University of Toronto, comments:

"I regard Da Free John as the most significant contemporary writer concerning the core of religion, more profound than Paul Tillich, Gabriel Marcel, and Martin Buber. Intimately acquainted with a vast range of spiritual experience, he peels off all externals and challenges us to join with him in surrender of our whole selves, shattering the egoism which contracts and separates us from participation in the loving, radiant life of God."[12]

Now that we have seen how people can confuse the medium with the message (castrating the latter merely on Da Free John's appearance), let us turn our attention to how the reverse can also happen. Several prominent thinkers have hailed Da Free John as a God realized Adept, a Divine Incarnation, the Avatar for the Western world, primarily on the strength of his numerous written texts. The problem in some of these ecstatic eulogies, though, is that they have been made without any direct personal observation of Da Free John, nor any experiential involvement with his methodology.[13]

What is occurring in many of these instances is a mere verbal assessment of Da Free John as a master based not upon intimate contact with him but on discursive reading. "He writes so well on the ultimate truths he must be a genuine guru." The danger in this approach is that we often end up measuring the competence of spiritual teachers exclusively on their ability to write or communicate well. Such a procedure is at best haphazard and inappropriately favors a left-brain inclination to religious leaders. If we judge masters in this way, and, no doubt, it should be an element in our appraisements, we leave ourselves open to an intellectual class of gurus versus a truly transformed group of enlightened men or women. A situation, I would add, that has led to the erroneous claims about Alan Watts' greatness. This, of course, is not to say that enlightenment and literacy are incompatible, but that the former should be adjudicated on evidence more than just the written word. There is no substitute for personal observation, involvement, or parallel experimentation.

It is readily apparent that some of the gracious praises for Da Free John's mastership are really for his writings. Yet, because certain writers confuse the message with the medium, they automatically link the two presuming that if one speaks eloquently about the transcendental reality he must also be a Seventh Stage Sage. This is not necessarily so.[14]

The authenticity of a religious teacher, though partially open to rational appraisements, is determined by the personal engagement of the student in day-to-day practice, sadhana, abhyas, or zazen. To secure judgments on anything less must be viewed as possible indicators of the teacher's status, not as final verdicts or endorsements.[15]

On the other hand of the scale, the legitimacy of a master's presentation can, for the most part, be adjudicated on the rational-verbal plane, as such an appraisement is chiefly concerned with the manifestation of the teachings on this level.[16]

Hence, while one may disagree with Da Free John's guru image (the presentation of his message on this plane), perhaps claiming that it has a low degree of legitimacy, no final judgment can be made on his authenticity until actual contact with him and/or his teachings is undertaken.[17]

This important distinction between authenticity and legitimacy, and the medium and the message, I believe, has not been made by many of those familiar, albeit slightly, with Da Free John's life and work. Either they dismiss Da Free John entirely because of his photographs or over hype him on the basis of his writings.

Interestingly, Da Free John's teachings or insight are not the controversial subject. Who, for instance, with any spiritual inclination, would deny that there is some greater power than us? That we have two fundamental options in the face of this Great Mystery: surrender or recoil? Or, finally, that God is Love and demands by His very existence that we participate via sacrifice of the ego in His Being? No, Da Free John's message isn't the cause for the debate surrounding him, it is his method of presentation, the legitimacy of his expression, which has turned admirers of his written word to harsh critics of his actions.[18]

Though there are really no good reasons to overlook Da Free John's vast contribution to spiritual philosophy and practice, there are some very pertinent questions to pose with regard to the validity of his organizational approach. Some viable criticisms that I have read or heard include: "His church charges money for membership; this automatically disqualifies it as a genuine spiritual movement by some standards. Do true gurus ask for money as a prerequisite for having audiences with them? Would Jesus request a donation?" "Da Free John has virtually no public ministry, save his contact with intimate disciples. This constitutes a cultic ring, a vicious circle wherein the legitimacy of the guru's actions goes unquestioned. Every blunder is rationalized, justified, or clarified as a "lesson for the devotee." "To be frank with you, though I am a follower of Da, I do get upset with how he is portrayed. Do we really need so many pictures of him?" "Personally, I find the Da to be more egotistical than causal. His constant use of I, though employed transcendentally, is quite condescending, especially if we are all `already happy/enlightened' anyway. Moreover, Da Free John makes absolute claims about his enlightenment and his unique way of presenting the essential truths. In a sense, if you take his argument to its full consequences, there is only one truly enlightened guru on the planet: himself! Everyone, according to Da, has their fifth and sixth stage limitations, except of course, himself. I find this not only presumptuous, but also an indication that it is not healthy to follow gurus who allege that they have attained something no other saint or yogi has."[19]

As for myself, though I am also critical of Da Free John's guru image and presentation (I have a resistance to any guru who charges money or makes personal claims about his own spiritual attainments.),[20] it does seem obvious to me that he is purposely invoking a parody of himself and all human teachers so that his reader/students may awaken from a purely intellectual perusal of his teachings and be confronted with the power of radical transcendentalism. I must admit that I never know what quite to expect from a Da Free John publication.

One year he is Franklin Jones, one-time disciple of Swami Muktananda, apparently extending the message of Advaita Vedanta for the western world; the next year he is Bubba Free John, the Spiritual Master, wearing Jewish styled caps; and in another year he is Da, with long hair, staff, living in seclusion, bald like a Zen monk, apparently much heavier, and preaching from a new island in the South Pacific."[21] Da Free John is, without question, the most iconoclastic teacher I have encountered. Not that his fundamental teachings change (they haven't), but that he continually upsets every model/label that he assumes. **Da Free John is literally like a Cracker Jack surprise in the religious world.** Just when you think that he has run out of new guises, Da Free John comes up with some bizarre clothing to startle you. [Check out the cover of his book, *The Bodily Location of Happiness* (2nd Edition), the picture of him on page 79 of *The Laughing Man*, Volume 4, Number 4, and the photograph of him in the book, *Nirvanasara*.] No wonder Da Free John has detractors calling him a cult weirdo; he invites such strong reactions by his selection of photographs.[22]

When Da Free John calls Seventh Stage Adepts crazy, he isn't playing semantic words games. He means it structurally: bodily, mentally and spiritually in contrast to the "norm" of our society and unenlightened man.[23] His "transmission" or "portrayal," depending on our estimation of his genuineness, upsets many of us, because true to his message Da Free John cannot adequately be pigeonholed.

Now this doesn't mean that we have to call him an enlightened being, or God-realized (can we really know if anyone is unless we ourselves are?),[24] but we shouldn't dismiss him in light of his teachings, as his writings do have an important spiritual import. True, Da Free John is a paradox, but he is at least a contradiction who elicits further examination of our own relationship with Reality.[25]

A Capsule Overview of Da Free John's Life

Unlike a number of his contemporaries in the guru world, who wish to conceal their past (e.g., L. Ron Hubbard), Da Free John is more open about his life.[26] Born on November 3, 1939, at Jamaica, Long Island, New York, with the given name of Franklin Albert Jones, Da Free John recalls that his infancy was marked with the "Bright," an a priori condition of enlightenment about the true nature of reality. However, because his family and the society to which he was born into did not enjoy that same "vision," Da Free John claims that he was forced by his circumstances to relinquish his Divine Communion. Elaborates Da Free John:

"When I was born there were no complications, there was no failure to understand, there was no lack of illumination.

But in my relations with family and friends it soon became apparent to me what kind of life is allowed in this world. It was obvious that my parents and their friends were unwilling to live as if they were in God and be happy. That was not permissible. So, obviously, I could not live that way either. I had to become their son and do the usual things that a child does, and, while doing that, continue to make the point of God-knowing."[27]

In the published accounts of Da Free John's life very little is mentioned about his childhood and early adolescent years. We pick up the narrative when he enters Columbia College in New York City at the age of seventeen. It was here that the "process of descending into ordinary life was complete--as a conventional human personality, Bubba [Da] was in a desperate condition."[28] Like ordinary men, Da Free John had to regain his prior understanding, where God (and not the ego) is the center and the circumference. He accomplished this by trying to "experience" whatever came his way. His quest had no limits; nothing was too baneful or too sacred. Yet, "neither his experiences nor his learning brought him closer to Truth."[29]

It was in the midst of this internal struggle that Da Free John allegedly experienced a spontaneous re-occurrence of "the Heart-Consciousness he had enjoyed at birth."[30] This regeneration, as it has been described, convinced Da Free John that freedom was native to man and not external to him. But, since this awakening was not stabilized, it too fell away and Da Free John persisted in his quest for permanent realization.

What was this hidden impulse that detained man from his already enlightened state? What force allowed man to persist in his egoic and suffering mood? The answers to these questions, which apparently haunted Da Free John for some time, became apparent to him in the early 1960's when he was attending Stanford University in California. As one "official" biographer puts it:

"He felt certain that there must be some hidden logic or force at the core of life that makes us abandon our native Divine Freedom for all the insane ways we suffer. To discover that logic, he had begun to observe and note in writing every single phenomenon that arose in body, mind, and environment . . . Finally it became apparent to him: The logic or principle of all birth, living, suffering, seeking, and death is hidden in the myth of Narcissus, the self lover of Greek mythology, who rejected relationship or love, in order to contemplate his own image, until he died. All human beings, he saw, live as Narcissus, locked into contemplation of their own selves, their own bodies and minds and destinies . . . ."[31]

After this breakthrough Da Free John returned to New York in June of 1964, where he subsequently met his first human guru, Albert Rudolph (more popularly known as Swami Rudrananda or "Rudi"). Along with his eventual wife, Nina, Da Free John sought tutelage under Rudi, who taught a physical version of Kundalini Yoga. [Rudi, it should be pointed out, was a follower of Swami Nityananda and his successor Swami Muktananda, both of whom resided in Ganeshpuri, India.][32]

Rudi's effect on Da Free John was perhaps more "preliminary" than transcendental, as he emphasized work and commitment, a grounding, so to say, for future spiritual development. At Rudi's insistence, Da Free John entered the ministry of the Lutheran Church. Though having no particular interest per se with Christianity Da Free John acquiesced and studied in the seminary for two years. But, as Da Free John recounts, while studying at the school he underwent a "death" experience, which culminated in the dissolution of his ego. Da Free John maintains that his experience was similar in content to Ramana Maharshi's, the famed Advaita Vedanta sage of south India.[33]

Propelled by his new insight, Da Free John shifted his discipleship away from Rudi to Swami Muktananda, and, in 1968, made his first trip to India to see the Siddha Yoga master. During his stay Da Free John became absorbed with the ascending currents of the higher radiant mind, which is "infinitely above the body, the mind, and the world."[34] For over a year, we are informed, Da Free John lived in a "distracted state, at times moved toward worldly experiences, and at other times moved toward the internal world. But from the time forward, Bubba [Da] was firmly established in a subtle level of awareness and Energy that transcended ordinary personality and character."[35]

Da Free John's contact with Swami Muktananda allowed him to directly perceive the various manifestations of the awakened kundalini: mystical lights, sounds, and other subtle phenomena. However, Da Free John was intuitively convinced that "Truth could not be equated with any kind of acquired experience."[36] Therefore, even Siddha Yoga as a method for God-realization was limited, since it was still concerned with "experiences"--albeit higher and more mystical ones. Da Free John felt that true realization was not the product of any one event, but rather the intuition of an already prior, coexisting, eternal state, which man had not lost but only "forgotten" in his ignorance.

In the summer of 1970 Da Free John finally achieved "permanent Re-Awakening" at the Vedanta temple in Hollywood, California. As he describes it:

"In an instant, I became profoundly and directly aware of what I am. It was a tacit realization, a direct knowledge in consciousness itself. . . I am reality, the Self, and Nature and Support of all things and all beings. I am the One Being, known as God, Brahman, Atman, the One Mind, the Self."[37]

After his "enlightenment," Da Free John realized that he no longer needed to meditate for his own sake. Instead, some other form of destiny began to work its power on him; this force was the karmic propensities of other unenlightened souls, who appeared naturally to Da Free John in his meditations. In a remarkable passage, Da Free John details what happened:

"After that time, when I would sit for meditation in any formal way, instead of contemplating what was arising in myself, I would contemplate other beings as my own form. Instead of my own psychic forms arising, the psychic forms, minds, and limitations of others would arise. I was aware, visually or otherwise, of great numbers of people, and I would work with them very directly on a subtle level."[38]

Led by this new destiny, Da Free John felt obligated to start teaching the spiritual path as it had been revealed to him. Thus, on April 25, 1972, after publishing his first book, *The Knee of Listening*, which was an autobiographical account of his quest and ultimate liberation, Da Free John commenced his public satsang on Melrose Avenue in Hollywood, inviting interested seekers to take up the practice of "radical understanding" in his company.[39]

In the beginning Da Free John's ministry was closely associated with Siddha Yoga and Advaita Vedanta, with pictures of Indian masters adorning the walls of his "Shree Hridayam Ashram." But, with his third trip to India in 1973, where he formally "sacrificed" his realization at various holy sites, and eventually severed his ties with Muktananda, Da Free John embarked on his own unique expression of the spiritual way. It was during this latter trip when Da Free John changed his name from "Franklin Jones" to "Bubba Free John" (lit., "a free man through whom God is Gracious").[40]

Then, in 1974, Da Free John and the staff of the "Dawn Horse Communion" moved to Clearlake, California, where they established a retreat sanctuary first called

"Persimmon" (later "Vision Mound Sanctuary" and now "The Mountain of Attention Sanctuary"). It was here where Da Free John began to work intensively with a small group of devotees, an inner circle in which to transmit his message of "Divine Ignorance" (formerly termed "Radical Understanding").[41]

After this intermediate and preparatory stage was completed, Da Free John "retired" from frequent public interaction with his general following and produced a number of source texts for his teachings, including such books as *The Paradox of Instruction, Breath and Name, Love of the Two Armed Form,* and *Enlightenment of the Whole Body,* etc.[42]

By the latter part of 1979, Da Free John changed his name for the second time (replacing "Bubba" with "Da," meaning "Giver"), and began the "hermitage" phase of his work, which enables him to live in relative seclusion. Presently, Da Free John lives with a small gathering of disciples (known as the "Hermitage Renunciate Order") on an island in the South Pacific called "Translation Island."[43]

Perhaps the most auspicious development in Da Free John's work has been the acknowledgement that several of his disciples have achieved "7th stage" God-Realization, which in essence is the same attainment that Da Free John himself secured in the Vedanta temple in 1970. This "collective" transformation is being heralded by the group as a milestone in the evolution of human consciousness, since it indicates that enlightenment can be the heritage of all human beings, not just the providence of a few rare individuals.[44]

Although the previous account only gives the salient features of Da Free John's life, it does bring us to the key issue in his teaching ministry: What constitutes genuine spiritual enlightenment? This question, more than any other, is the driving force in Da Free John's writings, for unlike most American gurus of his generation, he explicitly outlines the necessary hallmarks of true God-Realization.

The Spiritual Philosophy of Da Free John

"Since Truth is the Condition of all arising, direct Realization of Truth must be possible, essential, and necessary under ordinary or random present conditions, and not merely or especially under extraordinary or strategically attained conditions. It is not itself a matter of feeling energies, or seeing sights or visions, or of extraordinary hearing, or taste, or smell. Nor is it a matter of any thought, or projection into any kind of environment, high or low, subtle or solid. It is a matter of intuitive abiding in the unqualified condition on which the present conditions are a play."

--Bubba (Da) Free John,
The Paradox of Instruction[45]

Ultimate enlightenment, according to Da Free John, is not the by-product of any particular effort or scheme that man may devise, but is rather the very nature of reality itself throughout and beyond all conditions. Hence, true realization becomes more a process of re-awakening to the "Truth which is already the case" than a strategic effort for attaining some exalted goal. In a sense, Da Free John sees the intersection of God's absolute transcendence and His immanence meeting in the Heart of Man. Man's only real dilemma is that he blinds himself to the infinity of which he is an intimate part.[46]

A crude, yet perhaps accurate, example of Da Free John's lucid argument is that of the ocean and a bubble. The ocean, in our case, represents the total reality (God), whereas the bubble (self) exemplifies a seemingly limited existence. Now to the bubble it has two fundamental options: 1) surrender to the ocean which is the creator, sustainer, and destroyer of its separate life; or 2) recoil and live in the (illusory) belief that as a bubble it has a distinct, autonomous existence. True Self Realization, argues Da Free John, is when the bubble intuits its subservience to the ocean and that it has no real life except in relationship with the larger environment. Likewise, God Realization is when the bubble consciously and fully allows the ocean to live and inform its being.[47]

Ordinary man, drawn almost solely to his "bubble" existence, rejects out of fear the truth of his condition, attempting to find ways to prevent death (cessation of "separate" being) and prolong life (narcissism). The tragedy in such a plight is that it constantly overlooks what is essentially true, real, and eternal. Undoubtedly, losing one's self (bubble) in God (ocean) is a scary proposition, since it necessitates a complete letting go of attachments--be they gross, subtle or causal. But, even though the prospect "appears" frightening and sorrowful, giving up one's being to God increases the soul's (bubble's) capacity for enjoyment, happiness, and peace immeasurably as the Reality (ocean) is infinitely greater than man's finite conceptions.[48]

Thus, genuine spiritual life is a moment-to-moment understanding ("whole bodily," as Da Free John puts it)[49] of the truth of one's temporal life. Such a "radical understanding," though never an outcome of any one experience, has varying degrees of intensity and adaptation. To better illustrate this evolutionary progression, Da Free John refashioned the classic yogic chakra system into his unique hierarchical Seven Stages of Life, which attempts to portray both man's already developed state and his future potentials. Elaborates Da Free John:

"The stages of readaptation in this Culture of Resurrection are 1) the physical-vital, 2) the emotional-sexual, 3) the higher vital (the will) and the lower mental, 4) the truly moral, the higher mental, and the lower psychic, 5) the higher psychic, the cosmic "gnosis", 6) the Realization of the unqualified Condition of Consciousness, or the prior Freedom of the soul, and 7) the Sacrifice of the Awakened Self into the Infinite Radiance of God, or the Translation of the Soul of Man into the Divine Domain."[50]

Da Free John indicates that the first three stages (physical, sexual, and mental development) are the heritage and lot of common man. Few individuals have entered into the fourth and fifth stages (psychic/mystical maturation), and rarely progress onward to the sixth and seventh stages (Self and God Realization, respectively). Accordingly, Da Free John's proclaimed mission is to transmit, without obstruction, the very highest realization so that all men/women may share in their true Divine birthright.

Da Free John's philosophy has been given various titles throughout his career: Radical Understanding; Divine Ignorance; Radical Transcendentalism; and Advaitayana Buddhism. Yet, one recurring pattern stays the same; the ego is the root of man's ailments. Not that the ego is an absolutely indivisible part of a person, or that it is an identifiable "entity," but that man in his narcissistic retraction from infinity presumes (falsely) that his "Self" is located somewhere inside. In truth, argues Da Free John, there is no permanent ego, self, or soul, regardless of how spiritual one might become. Rather, what is real is the Transcendental condition out of which all manifestations arise. Identify with that True Reality, Da Free John contends, and genuine Enlightenment will occur.

Paradoxically, Da Free John's approach takes into consideration both the Buddhist (no-self) and Hindu (One True Self) perspectives concerning truth and points out how they are essentially two different expressions of the same fundamental reality. The Buddhist purview is "negative" (all objects, including God, are disavowed), whereas the Hindu outlook is "positive" (Brahman and Atman are one). Yet, regardless of emphasis, they are mutually interdependent correlatives, each giving a glimpse into the nature of man and the universe.[51]

One of Da Free John's strongest presentations to seekers concerns what he terms "Divine Ignorance." Put simply, it is the inability of a person to know what anything is. Writes Da Free John:

"What is Truth? I may find out or know all kinds of facts or truths about any thing, or everything, or the whole word. But I may never discover or know what that thing, or everything, or any thing is. No matter how much time passes, or how much knowledge is attained, this fundamental Ignorance can never be changed to any degree. This Ignorance is Truth and the Way of Truth. It is the Truth or Condition of any thing and everything. It confounds the dreams of knowing . . . "[52]

Although Da Free John's argument has several articulate precedents (e.g., from Kant's "we can never know the thing in itself" to Nicolas of Cusa's "The unattainable is attained through its unattainment")[53] its forcefulness and clarity make his elucidation irresistible.

Crazy Adepts and Sane Disciples

"Master Da Free John is not on an "ego-trip". Careful consideration will reveal that the ego that may be felt to arise while reading his writings is none other than the reader's."
--Fred Alan Wolf, Ph.D.[54]

Regardless of the beauty of Radical Transcendentalism, one cannot help but encounter a strong sense of ego in Da Free John's writings. Fred Alan Wolf in his Foreword to The *Transmission of Doubt* (see above excerpt) tries to explain this feeling away by arguing that it is the reader's ego which arises when reading, not Da Free John's. This statement, however, is logically inaccurate. For, given Wolf's argument, the opposite corollary should also be true: When the reader does not feel ego, it is because he/she is egoless.[55]

No, the actual truth of the matter (something which Wolf picked up on and tried to explain away) is that Da Free John's writings do reflect an egotistical stance. This is evident in his choice of language, the selection of photographs, the promotion of his exalted status, to finally the continuing advertising that his teaching is superior to any revelation prior to his advent. Da Free John may have transcended the ego and its constraints, but the presumptuousness of his books (vis-a-vis their style and promotion) is not simply due to the reader's lack of spiritual attainment or misguided apprehension. To put the blame on seekers when the "ego arises" is naive. Rather, the more appropriate explanation is that Da Free John has chosen to present himself, his teachings, and his organization in a format that invites skepticism. Is it simply the reader's ego that resists such Da Free John titles (essays and talks) as *A Birthday Message From Jesus and Me?*[56]

Though Da Free John alleges that he uses "I" and "Me" in a transcendental mode, its consistent use and juxtaposition with ultimate Reality has other effects. For instance, read the following excerpts from Da Free John's recent essay, *Pondering and Preparation*:

"The Way That I Teach is a Great Process. An Ordeal Of Self-Sacrifice to The Spiritual Form Of God. Many may Respond to My Offering, but some may need time to ponder and to prepare themselves. . . Those who find themselves in such a stage of Response to Me should not feel that they must remain apart from Me and the Fellowship. They should honor their Response to Me by becoming friends, patrons, and regular students of The Laughing Man Institute. . . Such individuals 'ponder' by engaging the sadhana of Listening to Me. . . by pondering My Arguments and Responding to My Person. Therefore, active patronage, friendship, student participation, and beginner's discipline are in fact forms of real practice. . . honored by The Fellowship."[57]

Perhaps the real "crisis" point at issue here is not only how one responds to the message of Radical Transcendentalism, but how one accepts Da Free John's transmission of the same. For those receptive to the "Crazy Wisdom Tradition," Da Free John's authentic voice may be sufficient for allegiance to his ministry. As James Steinberg explains:

"Because the Adepts are moved to immune and instruct whatever is brought before them, they may appear wild. They may appear self-indulgent, seem mad with powers, or act like fools. They may remain silent, or may teach through discourse or song, may appear angry, or warm, open, and loving. Historically, no two such Adepts were alike. Some practiced celibacy, and some were sexually active. For example, Marpa had one legal wife and eight Tantric consorts or partners. Yet his disciple Milarepa was naturally moved to be celibate. . . . "[58]

Furthers Da Free John: "But truly, actual Realization, the actual process, spontaneously produces dramatic changes in the psychophysiology of the true practitioner. Such an individual's behavior does change, both socially and in the way he or she teaches--and he would not teach as a monk sermonizes! Most of the teaching of such individuals is spontaneous, kind of wild and offensive. It typically shakes people up and offends them."[59]

However, for others concerned with issues of legitimacy (i.e., how the teacher/teachings are expressed on this plane), there may be some reticence to Da Free John. This "hesitancy" may include disapproval of his interaction with disciples, his self-proclamation about God-Realization, his requests for monetary subscriptions, and the "guru" image he portrays. Or, as Richard Grossinger points out in his review of *Easy Death,* even resistance to the name "Da Free John":

"I should emphasize that I have never met Da Free John nor been to his community or any of his centers. I know his teachings exclusively through the printed word. I began reading him several years ago because I was curious as to who this strange teacher was who had taken on the name of Bubba Free John (and then later Da Free John). I realize now that many people still wonder this and that the odd names keep them away. A number of potentially interested readers have turned away from these books on the false presumption that the name was an intentional parody of the role of guru or the clowning of a self-conscious guru . . ."[60]

We have now come full circle on the paradox of Da Free John. Unquestionably, he has presented a number of superb works on spirituality with unique vigor and insight, deserving of deep attention and respect. Yet, how one responds to Da Free John as a spiritual master depends upon a number of contingent factors, not the least of which concerns the connection between legitimacy and authenticity. In the final analysis, critical examination, while it is both beneficial and necessary, can only lead so far. Ultimately, the relationship between a guru and a disciple must result from a force beyond (but not necessarily versus) the rational mind. In the midst of that power, in the "fire" of that impulse, the student can test both the sincerity of his surrender and the genuineness of his master.

Thus, the paradox of Da Free John is in some ways the paradox of the disciple: an intricate koan between outward and inward signals. Perhaps the greatest irony of all is that for a master who writes so much about transcending ego, Da Free John should be labeled by a number of readers as an "egotist." But, even though we may not accept Da Free John's claim for mastership, we can at the very least benefit significantly from his writings, which convey truths so universal and penetrating that there can be no debate.[61]

Postscript | 1994

A few days after *The Paradox of Da Free John* was published in the early part of 1985, the *San Francisco Chronicle* and other Bay Area newspapers published an extensive expose of the guru's sexual exploits and violent interplays with female disciples. It was a significant blow to the group; some defectors even claimed that Da Free John had seven wives (the numbers vary, depending on the defector) and that he occasionally beat one of his wives. He is also reported to have had an alcohol and drug problem.

Although I had a very strong suspicion when I wrote *The Paradox of Da Free John* that the guru was having sexual relations with his disciples, their spokesperson at the time, Georg Feuerstein, assured me in writing that it was over and that when it occurred it was part of his spiritual theatre. The facts suggest something else was going on however. Indeed, Feuerstein was naively trying to gloss over his guru's transgressions by trying to put a "spiritual spin" on what was obviously unethical behavior for a normal person, much less a master who claims to be God-realized. Later Feuerstein tried to come clean about Da Free John when he left the group in the late 1980s. In his book, *Holy Madness,* Feuerstein tries to come to grips with Da's crazy wisdom approach. Feuerstein's effort, however, falls way short, since he does not reveal in-depth the scandals that hit the community or explain his own questionable actions at the time.

In retrospect, I think *The Paradox of Da Free John* is much too kind to the guru. True, Da Free John (now Da Avabhasa) remains a vitally interesting cult leader, but he has become so enmeshed in his own ego trip that it is nearly impossible for the reader to wade through his self-aggrandizing tirades and discover the rare philosophical jewel from time to time.

Furthermore, the unmitigated hype surrounding him and his mission has reached absurd levels, especially when someone as bright as Ken Wilber has the audacity to claim that Da Free John is the greatest spiritual master of all time and that his book, *The Dawn Horse Testament* is the greatest spiritual tome of all time. To be sure, Da has written some brilliant pieces, but to then extend beyond his writings into an ontological appraisement of his status in the universe not only seems completely arbitrary, but downright silly. One gets the impression that we are talking about comic book action heroes. Who is greater: Superman or Batman? Or, as Wilber would have us frame it: Da or Jesus? Well, the debate is entirely missing the point, something which Wilber has yet to come to grips with: brilliant writing does not make one a master. In fact, a great thinker may live a reprehensible life; and if the published reports of Da Free John are any indication of his personal integrity, then he ranks along with John-Roger, Thakar Singh, Paul Twitchell, and others, as a charlatan more bent on satisfying his personal whims than helping his disciples achieve their spiritual goal.

I say all of this in the context of someone who likes to read Da Free John's books. Da Free John is clearly a more important thinker than most of the cult leaders today, but that does not mean that we have to condone his mean spiritedness and immature taunts under the lame excuse of "Holy Madness." My sense is that if we leave out the adjective "Holy" we will get much closer to the truth behind Da Free John.

NOTES

1. There is a tendency when reading Alan Watts to presume that Enlightenment is an intellectual process; conceptually understand the ultimate truths of the universe and Self Realization naturally occurs. This is not correct, since genuine spiritual awakening involves the entire body-mind- soul complex. To intellectualize about Nirvana or Satori is quite easy, but to actually transform and surrender one's self to the Supreme Reality is a very difficult task indeed. For glimpses into Alan Watts' own trials and errors, see his autobiography, *In My Own Way*.

2. Although it is true that rituals have their place in setting up the right context for religious functions, it should not be forgotten that the essence of such superstructures, as Frits Staal (*Exploring Mysticism*) terms them, is to reveal (not conceal) the sacred mystery. All too often organized religions overlook their vital and primary purpose and begin to serve as social institutions concerned with purely ethical issues. It should also be pointed out here that not every seeker is attracted to a spiritual movement by means of the teachings. As Georg Feuerstein makes clear about the Johannine Daist Communion: "In our experience, people frequently join our Community not because of the Teaching but because of their response to the Spiritual Master. (They may have seen a photograph of the Adept or a video and subsequently read some of the literature.) The way in which potential devotees are "contacted" by the Adept is mysterious, and no reductionist explanation can do justice to what has actually happened in hundreds of cases and is continuing to happen to newcomers even now. This is not to deny that for many people the Teaching itself is inherently attractive, but we find that the Teaching literature is read by very many people who have made no attempt to take up this Way, presumably because they do not associate its attractiveness with the spiritual presence of the Adept. And those who are content to merely read the literature, many suffer from the illusion that reading

Master Da Free John's works is a sufficient form of spiritual practice. They belong to what the Adept calls the `talking school'."

3. In the M.S.I.A.'s worldview (i.e., John-Roger's novelistic creations), The Mystical Traveler of Consciousness is a force that has always been present on earth.

4. The history of M.S.I.A. is in many ways the life story of its founder, John-Roger Hinkins. John-Roger not only attempted to hide things about his past and cover-up his nefarious sexual activities, but he has also tried to set up phony smear campaigns against his detractors. See *The J.R. Controversy.*

5. The term "naive bumpkin" comes from Da Free John, as quoted by Georg Feuerstein in his Introduction to *Nirvanasara* (Clearlake: The Dawn Horse Press, 1982), page 8.

6. The cause for this change in attitude, I suspect, among disciples of Indian gurus has more to do with the student than with the teacher. For instance, when I was in India in 1981 I noticed that one Swedish seeker judged the greatness of a guru by how much time he gave to him personally. The result? If the master spent lots of time with him, he was a highly evolved teacher. If the master spent little or no time with him, he was still a struggling soul.

7. The bottom line in discipleship is that the student can never fully accept intellectually that his master is perfect. Hence, every absolute verdict or judgment that is made is always doomed to change or be radically altered. In this way, how a devotee sees his guru is to a large degree a reflection of his own inner struggle or advancement. However, there is also a certain element of constancy to a disciple's perspective, especially if they are mature practitioners. As Georg Feuerstein elaborates: "I can readily see that in a certain mood the Guru will appear to a

disciple in his transcendental nature, and in another mood the Guru will appear to him very mundane. But beyond these moods of the disciple, there is also a genuine heart intuition of the Guru's true nature that allows the disciple to understand his varying `readings' of the Adept-Teacher as projections. And that intuition deepens with his spiritual maturation, until the Guru is recognized to be literally identical to himself (or his Self), as the transcendental Being."

8. Since the tragedy of Jonestown there has been a great "cult scare" in America where any non-mainstream religious movement is suspect. In fact, though the word cult by definition is not pejorative it has become the mass media's buzzword for the religiously offbeat. This is unfortunate because there are a number of "cult" leaders who have some very insightful things to say about man, society, and God. Of course, this is not to overlook the glaring truth that many religious leaders are misguided or even dangerous.

9. The preceding quotations were selected from letters and interviews taken in the last ten years on the subject of Da Free John. Georg Feuerstein strongly objects to this type of "journalistic" writing on my part. Comments Feuerstein: *"[This section] is odious to me personally, because it promotes journalistic sensationalism. I merely want to comment on one point: The reason why Master Da Free John wears so many different hats is that all of them represent gifts from devotees, and he is wearing them for their sake, just as all his clothes are made and supplied by devotees. Without the notion of an Adept's perfect self-sacrifice, these gestures remain unintelligible. They are visible signs and the Adept is affirming his relationship with individual devotees constantly."*

10. Most of the anti-cult organizations today are religiously based. It is from a theological framework (usually Biblical) that such groups attack wayward religious movements, especially those that do not subscribe to their cherished

world-view. Again, I think this is a mistake. Even though we should be critically minded when studying new groups (as well as "old" ones), it is improper to dismiss penetrating ideas and thoughts simply because they do not fit into our own preconceived models of reality.

11. I would like to add that this particular student was exceptionally bright and went on to read parts of *The Paradox of Instruction*, as well as Ken Wilber's *Eye to Eye*. To the chagrin of my teacher associate, with whom I was a friend, the student won a major literary scholarship on the basis of a paper he wrote which quoted at length Ken Wilber's thoughts on the "perennial philosophy," portions of which contain elaborations of Da Free John's insights.

12. Quoted from the back cover of Da Free John's *The God In Every Body Book* (Clearlake: The Dawn Horse Press, 183).

13. There is often a tremendous amount of hype in spirituality. It is not dissimilar in some ways to the reviews of new Hollywood movies. If a recognized "reviewer" raves about a film, there is a predisposition among some movie-goers to question their own tastes. "Well, the *New Yorker* said it was a classic, so my boredom must be due to my inability to find the deeper meaning." Likewise, if a well known author in philosophy claims that a particular guru or master is "enlightened" the would-be reader is more likely to buy into it. The catch here, though, is that the writer may never have met the teacher in question. Furthermore, the philosopher may have some critical comments to make about the guru, but hesitates in doing so in fear that they will not be printed. Or, if such criticism is made the publisher does not include the same in the blurbs accompanying the book. The problem in all of this is that spirituality (or the guru's status) becomes a marketable item, polished and advertised to "look good," to be "acceptable" for the general reader. What is needed to counteract this "glossing sheen" is for individuals to directly find out what is occurring within the movement.

14. Georg Feuerstein sees my emphasis on distinguishing between the message and the medium as limited. Elaborates Feuerstein: "You make the point about separating the message from the medium. From a worldly (objectivist) and hence limited or partial point of view this is valid. However, from a spiritual perspective this separation of message and medium is a product of the materialistic mind that is unable to perceive the psychophysical unity of the cosmos. Thus, from the Adept's viewpoint, his Teaching is one of his Agencies and as such is co-essential with his spiritual presence and potency. His entire Teaching Argument is intended to bring people to a level of self-understanding that will then enable them to begin to relate to the Adept as Spiritual master. The Adept is the Way. But his esoteric equation is meaningless to the conventional mind that interprets reality on the basis of innate doubt and distrust. I agree with you that writing well is not a sufficient criterion for appraising a Teacher's authenticity. Master Da Free John is manifestly a marvelous writer, but his writings (most of which are in fact printed talks) have a communicative power that goes beyond niceties of style."

15. I owe this discussion of authenticity and legitimacy to the pioneering work of Ken Wilber. See *A Sociable God* and *Eye to Eye* for more information.

16. Georg Feuerstein and I disagree over the issue of legitimacy as a necessary criterion. My own feeling is that unless the master's actions are above suspicion on this plane, it is not wise to follow him in the spiritual planes. In other words, if you cannot trust the guru in the ordinary waking state, what assurances are there that he should be trusted in the spiritual worlds? Georg Feuerstein believes that the concept of legitimacy, as it is presently used, lacks sophistication, particularly in relation to authenticity. Writes Feuerstein: "Your comment that the `authenticity of a religious teacher, though partially open to rational appraisements, is determined by the personal engagement

of the student' is to the point. Precisely for this reason the sort of treatment attempted by you is of limited import. Its hermeneutical methodology necessarily suffers the limitations of the `outside' observer. Also, your sharp separation of authenticity from legitimacy is artificial. For instance, Jesus' well-known outburst of righteous anger at the money lenders in the temple cannot be legitimized other than by his authenticity as a Spiritual Master. If we assume he was less than an Enlightened Adept, then this act was egoic and not self-transcending, and the spiritual Principle cannot be thought to have been upheld by him in that case. Then the question of the legitimacy of his behavior can be appropriately discussed within the context of Hebrew mores. If, however, we see Jesus as an Adept, then his action immediately takes on a different significance. He may have acted out of keeping with standard behavior at a holy site, but a larger, spiritual Principle was involved that led to the immediate purification of the situation (that is, positive change in spiritual terms). Of course, the latter view only makes sense within a perspective that is nonmaterialistic. And, to be sure, such a non- materialistic orientation is essentially nonconventional."

17. It is extremely dangerous to make final judgments on any human attainment. Rather, we should always realize that our appraisements, though at times useful and necessary, are subject to revision. Moreover, since we do not have access to all levels of existence, it would be premature to make absolute claims on the nature of reality. As S.L. Frank beautifully points out in his landmark text, *The Unknowable*, the paradox of life is that the moment we know something with certainty, at that very same instant we do not know it. Every appraisement, even the one that is presented here, is but a partial glimpse.

18. Da Free John's work is exceptional. Though we may disagree with his guru image or even his lifestyle, it would be a mistake not to acknowledge the power of his writings.

Ken Wilber was not exaggerating in his praise when he wrote that Da Free John's *The Paradox of Instruction* "is, in its scope, its eloquence, its simplicity, and its ecstatic fund of transcendent insight, probably unparalleled in the entire field of spiritual literature." This book and others have rightly claimed an enthusiastic audience. The debatable point arises when we begin to equate superb writing/teaching with the author himself, particularly when there has been no personal contact or engagement with the guru.

19. These observations were taken from interviews and letters during the past ten years on the subject of Da Free John. Georg Feuerstein, again, disagrees with some of these comments, since he feels that they arise from a fundamental misunderstanding of the Adept and his work. Elucidates Feuerstein: "The question of legitimacy can obviously be used as a convenient instrument for the conventional mind to air its biases and presumptions. A good case in point is the whole matter of charging money for spiritual services. Money, like sex, has traditionally been regarded as being antithetical to true spiritual life. This naive view can be understood historically and psychologically. It is essentially neurotic, as is all purism. Besides, it is worth pointing out that the early Christian cult was entirely financed by its converts who had to give up all their worldly possessions! Jesus didn't request a donation, true. He demanded that his devotees or disciples abandon the world altogether and become renunciates. Naturally, they would not leave their possessions to the state, but make them over to the growing community of followers. Master Da Free John also requests no donation. Like Jesus or Gautama before him, he expects his devotees to live as renunciates in community with one another."

Personally, I have a different view than Georg Feuerstein on this subject of money. Perhaps it is my own prejudice but I remember when I was seventeen years old and went to one of Da Free John's (then Franklin Jones) public talks, where a group leader spoke on the teachings of his guru. The meeting was held in West Hollywood on Melrose Avenue during the beginning years of the movement (1973). Finally, after the presentation, an older woman raised her hand and asked how it would be possible to sit in formal meditation with Franklin Jones (Da Free John). The speaker answered by saying, among other things, that a donation of fifty dollars or more was necessary. Needless to say, this request for money was disconcerting to the audience that was present. My own views on this subject are outlined in "The Spiritual Crucible."

20. This notion of self-proclamation or gurus making claims about their own spiritual attainment is a complex issue. My own sentiments are in agreement with Julian P. Johnson's classic adage, "If any man claims to have attained the highest in spiritual development that claim of itself may be taken as conclusive proof that he has not attained so much." Georg Feuerstein has a different view. Argues Feuerstein: "2500 years have elapsed since Gautama the Buddha's parinirvana. 2000 years have passed since Jesus' crucifixion. Most of us now look upon both as truly great spiritual lights. Many regard both as fully Enlightened beings. And yet, both made personal claims about their own spiritual Realization. The New Testament is full of them, as is the Pali Canon. And let us not evade the issue by arguing that both documents do not represent the ipsissima verba of these two great Adepts. They may not give us the exact words of Gautama and Jesus but they certainly give us the gist of their Teaching and Work. Why should an Awakened being not proclaim his Realization if what is supposed to be his function is to make a visible impact on the world? Not every Enlightened being is destined to die in obscurity in a cave or a jungle. I dare say few are so destined."

21. The island is called Naitauba and is the location of the Hermitage Sanctuary of the Johannine Daist Communion.

22. Since Da Free John changes appearance so often (or at least in the pictures accompanying his books), it is understandable why "conventionally minded" readers are put off by him. To them, Da Free John looks like a caricature of the cult leader gone wild.

23. See Da Free John's *Scientific Proof of the Existence of God Will Soon Be Announced by the White House!* (Clearlake: Dawn Horse Press, 1980) for more on this perspective.

24. This is the inherent limitation of empiricism, rationalism, and even critical thinking. Regardless of how well we may analyze a situation when it come to spirituality or transpersonal realms of consciousness the investigator must engage in actual transcendent practices in order to rightly and fully understand the height of a teacher or master. This, of course, is not to say that rational scrutiny does not have its place (the existence of this essay is an argument for critical thinking), but only that we eventually move away from armchair speculations into experimental engagement. Georg Feuerstein is correct, I believe, when he states that my treatment of new religious groups has "limited import," since it suffers "the limitations of the 'outside' observer." However, even in its "limited" ability, such reports do serve a vital function in developing keen discrimination. Thus, the intellect should act as a stepping-stone for further evolutionary growth, not as a barrier or hindrance.

25. I think it would be unfair to categorically dismiss Da Free John and his writings, or, to lump him with the majority of other self-styled gurus in America. At the very least, though we may be critical of Da Free John's actions, etc., his writings do open us up to the utter Mystery and Wonder of creation. The directness of his argument is both refreshing and awakening.

26. It is curious, though, that Da Free John makes little or no mention of his parents/family.

27. Da (Bubba) Free John, *The Enlightenment of the Whole Body* (Clearlake: Dawn Horse Press, 1978), page 6.

28. Ibid., page 12.

29. Ibid., page 13

30. Ibid., page 13.

31. Ibid., page 13.

32. My biographical account here of Da Free John's life follows the information given in *The Enlightenment of the Whole Body* and *The Knee of Listening*.

33. For more on Ramana Maharshi's realizations see *Talks With Sri Ramana Maharshi,* Volume I and III (Tiruvannamalai: Sri Ramanasramam, 1972).

34. Da Free (Bubba) John, op. cit., page 19.

35. Ibid., page 20.

36. See Da Free John, *The Paradox of Instruction* (Clearlake: Dawn Horse Press, 1977) and *The Way That I Teach* (Clearlake: Dawn Horse Press, 1978).

37. Da (Bubba) Free John, op. cit., page 28.

38. Ibid., page 38. This excerpt is extremely important in revealing the impetus of Da Free John's ministry. If, as he says, psychic forms of other unenlightened beings began to spontaneously appear to him during meditation, it lends credence to why Da Free John felt moved to act as a spiritual master. Moreover, the passage is a pivotal revelation about how gurus are drawn to certain disciples. Apparently, there is a trans-structural destiny-awaiting individuals who transcend their own body/mind limitations. Instead of just merging totally with the

Supreme Reality, enlightened beings are propelled to "work out" the obstacles of other individuals who are karmically tied to them. Hence, contrary to our usual notions of spiritual teachers (and more in line with the esoteric interpretation of religious mysticism), a master is Divinely commissioned to function as an agency for liberating souls. This "commission," as it were, though, can only occur after one has completely freed the self from karmic/structural bonds.

39. Da (Bubba) Free John, *The Enlightenment of the Whole Body* (op. cit), pages 38-39.

40. Ibid., page 46.

41. The terms "Divine Ignorance" and "Radical Understanding" are used interchangeably and represent the Mystery behind all human endeavors for absolute knowledge.

42. With the publication of these texts, Da Free John's message became much more widely known (and, hence through extension, respected by scholars).

43. Roy Finch's article, The Most 'Phenomenal' Teacher, in Georg Feuerstein's (editor) *Humor Suddenly Returns* (Clearlake: The Dawn Horse Press, 1984), pages 63-74, contains some thoughts on the wisdom and necessity of Da Free John's move to the island of Naitauba.

44. See M-Fields: An Interview with Rupert Sheldrake, *The Laughing Man Magazine* (Volume 5, Number 3), for the possible ramifications of "collective enlightenment."

45. Bubba (Da) Free John, *The Paradox of Instruction* (Clearlake: the Dawn Horse Press, 1977), quoted from the back cover.

46. Da Free John eloquently points out that ego is not an entity but an activity. Hence, in reality it has no real or a priori substance. Rather, it represents the retraction (moment to moment) of man from his true and eternal condition (Oneness with God). See Bubba (Da) Free John's *The Paradox of Instruction* (op. cit.) for a more detailed explanation behind the egoic principle and its relationship to the Heart.

47. I have based my discussion here largely upon Da Free John's book, *The Four Fundamental Questions* (Clearlake: The Dawn Horse Press), which I strongly recommend as a good introduction to "Divine Ignorance" or "Radical Understanding."

48. Ken Wilber's books, *The Atman Project* and *Up From Eden* in particular, are excellent extensions of Da Free John's fundamental argument.

49. Da (Bubba) Free John, *The Enlightenment of the Whole Body* (op. cit.).

50. Da (Bubba) Free John's *The Way That I Teach* (Clearlake: The Dawn Horse Press, 1978) for an elaboration on these "Seven Stages of Eternal Life."

51. Da Free John, *Nirvanasara* (Clearlake: The Dawn Horse Press, 1982). Clarifies Georg Feuerstein: "Master Da Free John sees as his real Work the Teaching of the Yoga of Enlightenment, which has to do with the persistence of the Disposition of unqualified Love under all circumstances. In other words, Enlightenment itself is not the end state. It is a process, and a school."

52. Da (Bubba) Free John, *The Paradox of Instruction* (Clearlake: The Dawn Horse Press, 1977), page 30.

53. The most exhaustive treatment of the "philosophy of Ignorance" is S.K. Frank's masterpiece, *The Unknowable*. It is

considered by some scholars to be the most important work of 20th century Russian philosophy. Comments Georg Feuerstein: "It is important to realize that Master Da Free John's argument about Ignorance is not a philosophical proposition like Kant's or Cusa's. Its whole point is to throw the individual into just that Condition of Ignorance, to allow him to intuit It. So long as the Adept is understood as a mere philosopher and his Teaching as philosophy only, neither are really understood."

54. Fred Alan Wolf, Ph.D., Foreword, to Da Free John's *The Transmission of Doubt* (Clearlake: The Dawn Horse Press, 1984) page 11.

55. Simply put, the major criticism of Da Free John is the "appearance" that he is on an ego trip and that his writings reflect an exclusive revelation. For instance, there are a number of books written by other masters which do not give the impression of ego, e.g., *Talks With Sri Ramana Maharshi,* Paramahansa Yogananda's *Autobiography of a Yogi;* and Baba Faqir Chand's *The Unknowing Sage.* This "impression of humility" is not due to the reader but to the style with which the masters chose to express their life and teachings.

56. Although Da Free John writes so much about the oneness of God and that Enlightenment is our true condition/heritage, his language is distinctively dualistic, replete with "I" versus "you" statements. For some readers, this stylistic preference automatically removes them from Da Free John, as his tone is often paternalistic, and, in some cases, condescending. A good example of the latter is in the question/answer transcriptions between Da Free John and his disciples.

DEVOTEE: Bubba, you are communicating a consideration here to people who have not totally assumed it. But in the future we will be able to assume it.

BUBBA: It would seem that way, wouldn't it? But since I can never leave, it stands to reason that you can never change. Certainly you will all become better, but that betterness will be the ordinariness of that new time.

--Bubba (Da) Free John, *The Way That I Teach* (Clearlake: The Dawn Horse Press, 1978), page 243--

57. Pondering and Preparation, An Essay by Da Free John, August 25, 1984, *The Laughing Man Magazine* (Volume 5, Number 3), page 81. My personal problem with this particular essay, besides the overuse of "Me" and "I," is that the overall thrust of Da Free John's invitation involves some type of monetary subscription. For example, to be a "Friend" of the Johannine Daist Communion one should contribute $70 or more and subscribe to *The Laughing Man Magazine*. This continued emphasis on money as a prerequisite for "formal association," beginning in the early 1970's when a donation was expected for sitting in meditation with Franklin Jones (Da Free John), undermines the legitimacy of Da Free John's presentations.

58. James Steinberg, "Avadhoots, Mad Lamas, and Fools: the Crazy Wisdom Tradition," *The Laughing Man Magazine* (Volume 3, Number 1), page 68.

59. Ibid., page 101.

60. Richard Grossinger, *Far-West Journal* (November 1984), page 78.

61. Concludes Georg Feuerstein: "One final point: Although the Crazy Wisdom Adept constantly deals with the conventional mind of those who aspire to spiritual practice in his company, he NEVER pushes anyone beyond the point where he or she ceases to relate to the test with real understanding or self-insight, true surrender to God, actual reception of the Spirit-Current, etc. Besides, the disciple is always free to NOT participate, even in a verbal confrontation. The mark of the true Adept is that he will set

his disciples free, not bind them. But it is a mistaken popular notion that spiritual life is all sweetness and delight. It is a profoundly difficult struggle, an ordeal of constant self-transcendence. The other mark of any Adept worth his salt is that he will always provoke a spiritual crisis in his disciples or devotees. That hasn't changed in a thousand years!"

FINAL ADDENDUM

A number of years after I wrote *The Paradox of Da Free John,* I was approached by a one-time follower of Adi Da who (unannounced) came by to see me at Mt. San Antonio College where I had recently been hired as a Professor of Philosophy. This particular gentleman, very well known in the cult's inner circle (his girlfriend eventually became one of Da's wives) wanted me to dig deeper into the nefarious activities of his former guru. He presented me with a treasure trove of materials that cast Adi Da in a very disturbing and negative light. Around this same time, a number of disaffected disciples of Da sent me manuscripts detailing Da's abusive interactions with them. Each of them felt that Adi Da was a selfish and disturbed individual who (like his later counterpart, Andrew Cohen) was in dire need of long-term therapy or, worse, jail time.

Adi Da never did open himself up to public scrutiny and because of this he was surrounded by a group of sycophants who tended to please and placate his every whim. Ken Wilber rightly distanced himself from Adi Da, though not with the passion and vigor that many felt was necessary. In a personal letter to me, Ken acknowledged that Adi Da was a "fuck-up" (Wilber's exact words; not mine), even as he praised him as a pioneer in spiritual studies.

Too bad that Ken Wilber didn't learn his lesson from Adi Da and think more clearly and rationally before aligning himself with Andrew Cohen, another self-styled guru with a massive ego who systematically desecrated his relationship with his students. Narcissistic gurus, under the misleading pretense of "crazy wisdom," can justify any and all debasements. Giving someone herpes, as Adi Da was purported to do to one of his unsuspecting female devotees, isn't prashad or a sign of God's blessing. It is exploitation.

Perhaps the best way to keep one's critical faculties in tact when dealing with a so-called Master's questionable behavior is to ask one simple question: Would we accept the same conduct from an elementary school teacher interacting with our 8 year old child? Simply put, it is the disciple's responsibility to have a very high standard when it comes to his/her chosen guru or master. Otherwise, we become easy prey for charlatans and madmen who use spiritual entitlements for their own personal gain.

The paradox of Franklin Jones may be best summarized by using my appraisement and Ken Wilber's own words in proper juxtaposition: Adi Da wrote some brilliant books, but personally he was a *fuck-up*.

The Strange Case of Franklin Jones

Introduction

When I was asked by David Lane to write an account of my brief period as a member of the community centered around Franklin Jones (AKA Bubba Free John, Da Free John, Heart-Master Da, Da Love Ananda, Da Kalki, Da Avabhasa),[1] I was initially reluctant, for several reasons. I had been involved with the guru for only a few months back in 1974, and since that time we had followed widely different paths; I had taught middle school and eventually gone back to university, earning a Ph.D. in the History of Asian Religions, with a special interest in Classical Chinese texts. He had gone on to become a moderately notorious "cult" leader, living on a secluded Fijian island with nine "wives" and a small group of male disciples, supported by the earnings of a community of followers, mostly in the San Francisco Bay area, and the income generated by a string of increasingly monomaniacal, eccentrically written books, books that I had occasionally glanced through but had not read. Though I still regarded Da Free John as an intriguing and fascinating teacher, I had not bothered to keep up with his publications and exploits and was hardly current on his end of the guru business. It was not clear to me that I had any particularly interesting insights to offer or that my academic expertise gave me special qualifications to analyze the life and oeuvre of this puzzling man. Though my memories of my time in the community were colorful and potentially entertaining, I was never especially privy to dark secrets and my role in the ashram's history was utterly insignificant.

Furthermore, the methodological problems underlying this enterprise struck me as thorny, for while I am now a professional scholar of religion, I most certainly was not one in 1974. Back then I was a young university graduate embittered by the hypocrisy shown by an America at war with "communism" and its own children. I was not pleased at the prospect of a middle-class existence (assuming I survived long enough) and, like millions of others, was desperately trying to discover new ways of understanding that might make it possible to actually live the idealistic values with which I had been raised. The hopeful optimism of the late sixties was long gone by the dark days of 1974; it was time to stop browsing in the spiritual supermarket and get on with the serious work of inner transformation, before it was too late. The world was in dire straights and nothing short of a revolution in human consciousness could hope to save it, desperate times requiring desperate measures.

Like many of my apocalyptically anxious fellow-travelers, I was fairly immature, reasonably cynical in a generic way, but at the same time quite naive and impressionable in specific instances. I suppose I was reasonably representative of an entire generation of individuals, who despite their many differences shared similar attitudes of frustration, despair, and longing. For many, the answers were no longer to be found in the failed theologies and empty religious practices of the West. We looked East for the ecstatic awareness that would halt the mad march of consumer "culture," heal the planet, and restore our souls. What made sense to us then may seem very strange in the 1990s. In the process of mulling over my experiences, I have been reminded again and again just how subtly, but significantly, my current frame of reference differs from that of twenty years ago; the same must be true for nearly everyone, which leads me to suspect that projecting oneself into one's own past is nearly as perilous an undertaking as predicting the future.

What finally convinced me to write this essay was the realization that my experiences of Da Free John, though brief, occurred at a time of unusual openness. Although the guru has been extraordinarily reclusive for many years now, when I was in the community he was relatively accessible, and his activities were in plain view. With hindsight, it is clear that in 1974 Da Free John was planting the seeds of behaviors that would grow into luxuriant, noxious weeds in the tropical isolation of his Fijian hideaway. With luck, my narrative of the early days of his community in northern California might shed some light on the later developments that were at least partially revealed in a series of investigative articles published from 4 to 16 April, 1985 in the *San Francisco Chronicle*.[2]

The most intractable methodological question may be this: how does an academic in the 1990s reconstruct the experiences had by an alienated, naive spiritual seeker nearly two decades earlier, without taking advantage of hindsight and the information and understanding gained in later years?[3] A secondary question concerns the proper tone and style for presenting this account. Should I pretend to be a "serious" scholar and write in formal academic prose? Would this not be absurdly pompous and inappropriate, given the material? Should I simply report on my memories, fighting down the urges to editorialize, moralize, and analyze? (in that priority!)

It seems to me that for this account to have any value whatsoever I will have to be as open and direct as possible. This will preclude any pretense of academic distance or "objectivity," especially since pretending to be a disinterested observer, when it is obvious I was not, will not fool anyone and will give an eerily detached tone to the essay.[4] At the same time, I will not be satisfied merely to report my experiences without comment or self-defense, especially since I am bound to look pretty foolish in these memoirs! As a compromise, I will present a straightforward, albeit impressionistic, account of my experiences in the Dawn Horse Communion (as Da Free John's community was then known), trying to interpret and present events as they appeared to me at the time, and follow with my analysis. When I cannot refrain from commenting, I will try to restrict myself to the notes, though some in-text editorializing will be unavoidable. Can this be justified on rigorous methodological grounds? Probably not, but perhaps the tale will prove entertaining and have some cautionary value.[5]

As a final methodological concern, I should address the issue of the *ad hominem* argument—not in order to make deep theoretical points but simply to clarify what my operating framework will be. It is an unquestioned axiom in graduate school that the *ad hominem* argument is invalid; you cannot refute a person's logic by attacking his or her character, race, religious beliefs, etc. One can think of many examples to illustrate this point. The Nazis dismissed Einstein's theories because he was a Jew; while this turned out well for the Allies, it was bad science and bad logic. We presumably all agree that the sexual mores of a chemist will not necessarily affect the results of her laboratory experiments, and the truth of an astronomer's cosmological speculation is largely independent of his personal hygiene; however, on entering the arena of normative pronouncements, statements of what is ultimately true, the questions get stickier.

If a Belgian academic claims that texts have no meaning other than that imputed to them by their readers is it relevant to note that he wrote Nazi propaganda during WWII? Does the *ad hominem* argument have bearing on this academic's truth claims? Obviously, being a Nazi propagandist does not invalidate one's theories on texts and their meanings; the logic of the claim is not refuted in any way by the *ad hominem* arguments leveled against its proponent, however is it improper to wonder about the psychological motives that might lead this particular academic to make the claims he does, claims that appear to absolve authors from any responsibility for what they write?

In the field of religion, especially when considering the role of charismatic, authoritarian religious leaders, the validity of the *ad hominem* argument becomes an even more important consideration. While character examination may never undermine the logic of a spiritual leader's positions, I suspect it may well be the most appropriate means to evaluate a guru, or any other teacher claiming divine inspiration for his or her actions. In other words, I believe that the *ad hominem* argument is potentially the most useful (though perhaps the most misused) means for evaluating religious or spiritual claims. Why?

In all of the world's major religions there are sub-traditions that emphasize the paramount value of the spiritual preceptor (*guru, rebbe, murshid, shih-fu, roshi,* etc.) These traditions claim that the spiritual preceptor can greatly accelerate the development of the disciple who submits completely to the preceptor's will.[6] In addition, they generally caution that the right preceptor is necessary for growth; a fraudulent or deluded preceptor is disastrous for the disciple and can literally ruin his or her spiritual life. Since the choice of preceptor is so important for the disciple, the traditions have cautioned the spiritual seeker to be highly critical when selecting the man or woman to whom he/she will entrust his/her life and have taught criteria by which true teachers are to be recognized. Besides emphasizing the importance of common sense and intuition, the criteria usually include a critical examination of the moral quality of the preceptor's life. As Jesus is quoted as saying in a related context, "By their fruits you shall know them."[7]

What these traditions seem to understand (or perhaps never had to consider) is that the distinctions modern persons make between spheres of action–physical vs. mental, spiritual vs. material, academic vs. personal, intellectual vs. moral, etc.–are both arbitrary and inappropriate when considering spiritual teachers. As these teachers usually claim, there is no spiritual world divorced from everyday life. The preceptor, or guru, claims the entire life of the disciple as his/her field of action; there is no area of the disciple's life free from the scrutiny and correction of the guru. Taking this claim at face value, it only follows that every aspect of the guru's life is also open to the critical examination of the disciple; there is no life of the spirit divorced from everyday human interactions and mundane concerns. The intellectual work of an English professor may be separate from his sex life,[8] but a guru's is not. Given the inseparability of spirit and matter, the cosmic and mundane, what more relevant way is there to evaluate a teacher than by his or her relationships with persons, possessions, and the environment? While I will do my best to avoid all questionable, unsupported allegations, I will not hesitate to discuss actions taken by Da Free John that seem to bear directly on the question of character.[9]

It is my belief that spiritual liberation does not free one from all rules of conventional morality. Though it is obvious that social mores are made up, the creation of particular human societies, and may well be hypocritical, inconsistent and arbitrary,[10] does it necessarily follow that the individual who is "liberated" is free to indulge in what appear to be egocentric, hurtful, and damaging actions in the name of spiritual freedom? I personally think not, while acknowledging the subtlety and complexity of the ongoing debate.

THE COMMUNITY

In March of 1974 when I arrived in San Francisco, the Dawn Horse Communion was in a period of rapid change and growth. The community had recently moved from Los Angeles, was acquiring a more formal structure, and, on the strength of Franklin Jones's first two books, was beginning to attract new members from areas outside California. (Even so, the group was still quite small, numbering fewer than two hundred, I would guess.) Within a day or two of my arrival from Colorado, a

Canadian appeared, having hitched rides all the way from Ottawa. As trivial as this may sound, the appearance of new prospective members, coming from distant cities, was interpreted by the rank and file members of the Communion as a strongly confirmatory sign and a harbinger of growth to come–their guru was finally being recognized by the outside world and spiritually receptive people were being drawn across the continent.

The timing of my arrival was quite fortuitous. Da Free John had recently begun the process, apparently still evolving, of distancing himself from the rank and file of his ashram. New members were required to pass through a probationary period of six weeks or more before being allowed into the guru's presence. For some reason, the persons who arrived the week I did were immediately accepted into the community and were allowed to join full members on the weekend pilgrimage north to "Persimmon," formerly Seigler Springs, the down-at-the-heels hot springs resort that was then the home of Da Free John and his select inner circle. Individuals who arrived only several days after I did were required to pass through a trial period of several weeks or months before being allowed to see the guru, and if I remember correctly there were even several luckless souls who had arrived before I had who were still held to the requirement of a probationary period. To this day I have no idea why the rules were relaxed for several of us, unless it was the feeling of exhilaration and unfolding destiny that gripped the community when we arrived from thousands of miles away. In any case, the rules were soon to be reasserted; by the time a few months had passed, all the "privileged" newcomers had either been expelled or demoted to the level of probationary members.

The contact point for spiritual seekers interested in learning more about Da Free John was the Dawn Horse Bookstore on Polk Street in San Francisco. This was where the other new arrivals and I met with more established members of the ashram and found housing in the community. I do not think that there was any master plan dictating this role for the store, rather events unfolded in an organic, ad hoc manner–the store was highly visible, staffed by community members who were friendly and desired to assist newcomers, new housing arrangements were being made as members moved up from L.A. to the Bay area, etc.

I was soon living in an apartment with an older couple (both were approaching thirty!) who had been students of Swami Satchidananda for most of the previous decade, sharing a room with the aforementioned Canadian, an ex-follower of Yogi Bhajan. In this arrangement, the Canadian and I were clearly junior partners; the older couple had been around the spiritual scene far longer than we had and knew the gossip on gurus and spiritual teachers up and down both coasts. More importantly, they were apparently fairly close to Da Free John. While not quite members of his inner circle–those privileged individuals who lived in his house or at least got to stay full time at Persimmon–they were still regulars at the guru's parties and seemed to have an inside track on the gossip about the guru on which the community throve. Besides tantalizing us with tidbits of information we really should not have been told, the older couple also helped us adjust to the rigorous diet and hygiene requirements imposed by Da Free John on the rank and file.

Da Free John was apparently fascinated and persuaded by the claims of various health food enthusiasts, so much so that he often stated that the neurotic symptoms of modern Americans, rather than pointing to deep underlying existential concerns, are merely trivial, the byproducts of bad diet and its accompanying metabolic disturbances. "Your deepest worries and spiritual traumas are just 'lunch'" was his metaphoric way of phrasing it. Furthermore the guru had no reservations about experimenting on his followers.

When I arrived, Da Free John's favorite diet authority appeared to be Paavo Airola. All members of the community[11] were required to follow Airola's prescriptive routine of a strict vegetarian diet, complemented by fasting one day a week, with a monthly three-day fast thrown in for good measure. Once a year, the community was expected to fast for a week, their only calories coming from watered fruit juice.[12] To accelerate the cleansing process, those fasting were also expected to take daily enemas, a novel experience for most of us. While this strict diet and periodic fasting were being observed in San Francisco, the guru and his fluctuating, but small, inner circle appeared to be engaging in increasingly riotous, drunken parties.[13]

Members of the community were required to write spiritual journals in which they recorded their experiences in meditation, doubts, hopes, growing love for the guru, feelings of surrender, and the like. These journals were collected weekly and read by a "big brother" or "big sister," assigned to each member by someone higher up in the organization. I do not remember, or perhaps never knew, how these assignments were made, but do recall noticing that that the men and women responsible for reading the journals and socializing newer members seemed to be selected from among the most loyal and unquestioning members of the "old guard," disciples from the ashram's Los Angeles days. It quickly became apparent that honesty in our journals was not a virtue to be rewarded; any expression of doubt, confusion, or uncertainty led to long, unpleasant probing from the higher-ups and the suggestion that perhaps we were not "mature enough" as disciples to deserve the experience of spending weekends in the master's presence. Our entries soon became formulaic and unrelentingly enthusiastic, loaded with the jargon of surrender and grace. It was also suspected that really powerful journal entries, if sustained long enough, might lead to improved standing within the community and eventually lead to greater contact with the guru, the goal of all good disciples. In this manner we were encouraged to express our love and devotion for the guru again and again, in many different ways.[14]

Meditation, practiced twice daily, posed another demand on our time, though it was one of the more enjoyable parts of our routine. We were instructed to sit before a picture of Da Free John–a great number of them were available for purchase–periodically asking ourselves "avoiding relationship?" The practice was not supposed to degenerate into mechanical repetition, but for me anyway, it did not lead to ecstatic states of consciousness or even a strong sense of connection to the guru. What it did for others, I cannot say; when I earnestly enquired what the point of this practice was supposed to be, senior members of the community seemed baffled and questioned my devotion, so I quit asking before I had an answer. In any case, it was pleasant enough to sit quietly for a stolen half hour of rest.

Overall the mood was exciting, fraught with anticipation of the profound spiritual revolution beginning before our very eyes. There was a strong sense that we were on the vanguard of a new spiritual order, that personal transformation was occurring all around us, by the grace of the guru. Since Da Free John worked his transformative magic by means of a mysterious process of osmosis, or transference of enlightenment, the highest priority of everyone was to gain access to the guru. This led to utterly embarrassing attempts to ingratiate ourselves with those in power. The greatest power lay with those who controlled access to the master, so nearly every member of the community vied to please these sternly right-thinking individuals by appearing to be the most surrendered, pious, obedient, hard-working, etc., devotee of all time.[15] One result of this attitude was that a great deal of work got done. In addition to holding full time jobs, community members were expected to spend every evening from Monday to Friday at the bookstore, where work, talk, and inspiration went hand in hand. We built and finished a warren of offices and meeting rooms in the leased space adjoining the bookstore in San Francisco and worked weekend wonders on the decrepit buildings of Persimmon, rebuilding them when possible, demolishing them when not. Safety was never a concern, since it was understood that the guru's grace was protecting his disciples at all times. We ripped out asbestos tiles and threw them into great dusty piles; we stood on steeply sloping roofs, tearing shingles loose like madmen. It worked out well for a while, though I was saddened to hear that one of the most ardent and surrendered disciples fell from a ladder, to his death, soon after I left. Even this tragic event held a strange salvational lesson for the community; Da Free John placed his hands on the dying boy and directed his soul through the stages of the afterlife, presumably securing liberation or at least a better rebirth for him.[16]

At the end of a long day of work, meditation, and lectures, there was still time for a bit of fun; after all, Persimmon had been a resort in several of its earlier incarnations. A favorite amusement was to run off to the hot springs, actually a series of pools, varying in temperature, in separate dimly-lit rooms, housed under one roof. Here my friends and I felt constrained by our liminal standing in the community (and our aesthetic sensibilities). Probationary members were expected to maintain celibacy, while full members were allowed to engage in "mature, responsible sexual relations" (apparently a euphemism for exuberant promiscuity). My cohorts and I fit neither category and never clearly knew where we stood, though it was obvious that remaining celibate was the safest course. In any case, despite its sybaritic possibilities, cavorting naked in the hot springs proved to be no more erotic than same-sex bathing at a seedy summer camp. Given the intense sexual/spiritual charge permeating nearly all aspects of ashram life, this seems almost inexplicable, but it is true. In dozens of hours of nude bathing, I saw nothing more sexual than occasional displays of affection. Perhaps the decaying, vaguely unsanitary, mildewed atmosphere of the baths kept things under control, by reminding everyone of junior high school swimming lessons. More important may have been the fact that my friends and I were actually repelled by most of the women in the community, who despite being former hippies managed to project a cloying, saccharin air of pious guru devotion. I felt like I was skinny-dipping with nuns. Late at night, I was told, the guru and his senior disciples occasionally staged drunken orgiastic revels at the baths, but by then we worker bees were safely tucked into bed and lost in dreamland.

Between jobs, commuting, housekeeping, hygiene (remember the enemas!), meditation, and work on the bookstore, our days were very full; most of us had little time for sleep, and I recall that I was hard pressed to do the reading and writing demanded of a new community member. In fact, I was hardly able to read at all during this period, despite my own inclinations and the guru's expectations. Whether this was the intended result of our schedule, I do not know. Perhaps the needs of a growing community dictated our excessively long workdays; possibly Da Free John wanted his followers to be too busy to think. One can imagine motives, both benign and nefarious, for encouraging our frantic lifestyle; while the effect of all this busyness was to forestall critical thinking, who can say what the guru's intentions might have been?

THE INNER CIRCLE

The first fact I should state about the inner circle is that I am not really qualified to speak about it, or rather that I have no first-hand observations to report about what went on inside the guru's home. What I can detail are my own observations of the dynamics of the guru's household, as seen from outside, and my remembered conversations with those who had direct access to the guru in his less public role. As already mentioned, I also had an earful of guru-centric gossip, a source that is not to be disparaged in ashram settings.[17]

Da Free John was in his mid-thirties in 1974, tending towards obesity but still muscular and fit. While not strikingly handsome, he was reasonably attractive and dressed with a free-spirited flair. His most intimate associates were roughly his age or perhaps a bit older. He appeared to be especially close to two men; the core of the inner circle seemed to be formed by the three men and their wives, though even members of this tiny elite were not immune to periodic banishment into the outer wilderness of the rank and file.[18] In addition to this core group, there were usually several single men, notable mostly for their arrogance and expensive sunglasses, who flanked the guru like bodyguards when he went out, and a half dozen or so attractive, ethereal younger women, collectively known as the "gopis," making up the inner circle.[19] The members of the inner circle did not appear to work, at least not at the heavy demolition and construction that occupied most weekend hours for the rest of us, and were greatly envied by everyone else. However, it appears that they paid a heavy price for their relative ease.

Like many gurus, Da Free John worked to undermine all attachments between individuals; ultimate allegiance is to the guru alone, for other relationships are driven by unhealthy desires, insecurities, cravings, and the like, that must be transcended before liberation can dawn. To this end, Da Free John ruthlessly separated couples he deemed too attached to one another, sometimes dissolving marriages or dictating that new relationships be formed.[20] The guru also had sex with a large number of attractive women. This was hardly a secret, especially since many of the women so favored had no qualms about telling others the details.[21] It was my distinct impression that Da Free John was already physically abusive towards women, pushing and slapping them around on occasion. This is hard to document, of course, since the apparent abuse was always interpreted and reported in the context of *shaktipat*, the imparting of divine energy or grace through physical contact, among other ways.[22] One woman in her first trimester of pregnancy told me how Da Free John had ordered her to down a drinking glass full of Aquavit, a vile Scandinavian liquor; he subsequently punched her swelling abdomen. She experienced this as a blessing given to her unborn child. Not surprisingly, the unusual sensations she felt were interpreted as the working of the *shakti*, or spiritual energy.

While the inner circle remained relatively constant during my stay at the ashram, I did see two women make the big leap into the limelight, in dramatically different ways: one quite unintentionally; the other through audacity and guile. The first instance occurred several weeks after my arrival, when the restrictions on visiting Persimmon and seeing the guru were being tightened. A recently graduated physician with a long-standing interest in meditation and eastern spirituality brought his young blond girlfriend into the bookstore one evening and enquired about seeing Da Free John. Officially, of course, this was now impossible; all new members had to adopt the prescribed diet and lifestyle changes, demonstrating their spiritual maturity for many weeks, before they were deemed adequately prepared to meet the guru. However, quite inexplicably, someone thought to call Da Free John and consult with him on the matter. After hearing the beauty of the girlfriend described in glowing terms, an exception to the new rules was suddenly granted, and the couple joined the weekend caravan to the hot springs. By this time I had had an opportunity to converse with the young woman, discovering that she had little or no background, or even interest, in eastern spirituality, meditation, and similar matters, and was only going along to humor her boyfriend. The next time I saw her she was wearing a sari and wandering glazed-eyed in the garden fronting Da Free John's house.[23] As it turned out, upon their arrival the visiting couple had been ushered into the master's home, where a party was being held, apparently in their honor. By Saturday morning, she had become one of the resident "gopis," and the young doctor was gradually being eased out of the house. On Monday he was back in San Francisco, presumably contemplating the spiritual anguish that inevitably arises from sexual attachments and failure to surrender wholeheartedly to the guru.[24]

The second case involved a rather nondescript, but not unattractive, woman who came to the community in the aftermath of a divorce. This woman quickly realized where the power and status in the ashram were concentrated and began plotting to become one of the guru's consorts. To those of us who observed her pathetic maneuvering–new makeup, flowing silk gowns and saris carefully selected to mimic gopi-wear, rushing to sit in the front row during meditation and talks by the guru, pushing to be near the guru on his daily strolls, outrageously fawning behavior, etc.–her apparent failure to attract the guru's attention was gratifying; perhaps the guy really was omniscient, or at least had good taste. Although posturing and positioning are integral aspects of guru-based community life, this woman brought a new level of transparent desperation to the process. One week, back in San Francisco, we noticed a change in her behavior; everywhere she went she carried a pen and paper and was observed writing and rewriting with great intensity, working on a manuscript the length of several term papers. It soon got out that she was composing a letter to Da Free John, a letter through which all the love and devotion in her heart could flow directly to the guru, unimpeded by the censoring tiers of ashram bureaucrats that separated ordinary community members from their lord and master. Somehow the letter was delivered–no mean feat in itself, for Da Free John's house was strictly off-limits–and the guru was moved by her great sincerity; the next weekend she was wearing her own sari and had moved into the guru's house, the oldest of the gopis. By the time I left the community, it appeared that her blissful smile was a bit forced, and she was showing signs of strain, though no one knew its cause.

THE GURU

When discussing Da Free John there is strong temptation to use that much debased word "charisma" to explain his personal magnetism.[25] To say that he has enormous charisma tells us little, however, since the apparent power and magnetism displayed by certain gifted religious and political leaders cannot be scientifically measured and will not be subjectively perceived in the same manner by different observers. How many of us would have come away from a face-to-face meeting with Jim Jones convinced that he was God? Yet for some individuals he had that level of persuasive power, and even his critics reported being swayed by his charm. In a similar fashion, Da Free John projected an almost palpable aura of certainty and self-confidence that seemed utterly remarkable in one so young. Whereas everyone else I knew was baffled by the big questions of human existence–Who are we? Why are we here? What does it all mean?–Da Free John was a man with answers, all the answers, and he was not simply a glib talker. His answers made perfect sense, fitting together like the pieces of an exquisitely crafted puzzle, once you accepted his basic underlying suppositions. I suspect that for someone hostile to Vedantic teachings and their assumption that souls reincarnate for lifetime after lifetime, until escape is won with the dawning of the supremely ecstatic experience of enlightenment, Da Free John's talks would have little power or appeal. For seekers already steeped in Indian spirituality, Da Free John's early talks are astonishingly well reasoned, encyclopedic in their breadth, impeccable in their logic, and, most importantly, clearly grounded in deep personal experience. When he gave his masterful lectures, without notes or other signs of advanced preparation, I was absolutely positive that he was speaking from his own experience, not parroting memorized lines.[26] To this day, I remain convinced that Da Free John could have spoken with the authority he displayed only because he was discussing vivid personal realizations.

On a sweltering afternoon in late spring, Da Free John might set out on a leisurely walk around the grounds, surrounded as always by an adoring crowd of dewy-eyed disciples. Despite being a healthy young man, the guru usually carried one of his collection of walking sticks, perhaps because many Indian sadhus walk with staves. Besides his designer sunglasses, he often wore nothing but sandals and a shawl; in a more modest mood he might wear colored bikini-style briefs, but nudity was his norm in the heat. Sometimes, after strolling a few hundred yards, he would sit down on a chair or blanket and appear to enter an ecstatic state of open-eyed trance, staring fixedly into the eyes of his followers, one after another. Soon others would enter altered states of consciousness, apparently drawn by the force of the guru's meditation. On occasion, individuals would assume difficult and contorted yoga postures, as the energy surging through their bodies compelled them to move and writhe. At other times the mood would grow incredibly quiet and still. An hour might pass like this before the guru would look up and ask, "Any questions?" Someone would then ask a silly question (soon forgotten)[27] and the master would launch upon a brilliant explication of some obscure technical point in Kashmiri Shaivism, or western occult theory, or his own superior understanding of Truth, or whatever; it really did not matter. We all loved to hear his spellbinding, illuminating, and eminently sensible descriptions of the real spiritual life that dawns with the end of seeking and suffering, for that was the ultimate destination of most of his talks. Da Free John's best discourses were reserved for formal meetings in the meditation hall, where his words could be taped for eventual publication, but even in the most impromptu settings he never seemed to stumble, make mistakes, lose a train of thought, or display ordinary human weakness. In my opinion, his act would be almost impossible to imitate.

When he was scheduled to speak in the ashram's lecture hall, we would assemble early, most people struggling to get as close to the guru's chair as possible, several of us with attitude problems sitting in the back row, as if still in school. We would usually meditate quietly until Da Free John made his dramatic entrance, encircled by the fluttering gopis. The effect was often startlingly electric. These were strange days, even by ashram standards, and the *shakti,* or spiritual energy, seemed wild, almost uncontrolled. Individuals would writhe or cry out with eerie animal voices as waves of delirious exultation swept through the room. Suddenly, Da Free John would quiet the crowd and, seating himself on his elevated throne, begin his discourse. To get a sense of the structure and content of these talks, one need only glance through *The Method of the Siddhas* or *Garbage and the Goddess*. So far as I can tell, Da Free John is unique among gurus, in that his books present his discourses in a completely unrevised, unedited form.[28] What you read is a word-for-word transcript of his talks.

During his lectures, Da Free John repeatedly, eloquently, and humorously attacked the narcissistic self-absorption that he claims has overshadowed our original enlightenment and become our habitual state of consciousness. Only by understanding and transcending our petty attachments, dropping our egos, and free-falling mindlessly into the sheltering arms of God can we recover the ecstatic, unreasonable happiness that has been our true condition all along. The way to reach this state of supreme happiness is to surrender to the guru at all times and in all situations.

As Da Free John spoke, his eyes would rake the crowd. Curiously, he appeared to make extended eye-contact with every member of his audience, no matter how many individuals were present.[29] On occasions when the mood hit, he would enter a silent state of meditation that would then flood over the assembly. When he had finished speaking and answering questions, he would abruptly rise and walk out, followed by his scrambling entourage. The rest of us would slowly collect our wits and trickle out into the warm, dark night.

Although Da Free John was most impressive, he was not at all approachable; he had no friends. Everyone was his student and everyone needed to be prodded, poked, cajoled, tricked, and even tortured into surrendering the attachments that prevented them from living the blissful enlightenment that was their true, already existing state. At the time I wondered what it would be like to have no peers, to be beyond correction, to admonish others but never to be admonished oneself, and concluded that one could only remain sane if one were "fully enlightened." Anyone less than a "perfect master" would be certain, I reasoned, to end up like one of those loony, sadistic pedophile emperors from the declining years of Rome.

In retrospect, I suppose that Da Free John was already losing his balance; he certainly seemed to enjoy stripping persons of their "attachments" with an enthusiasm that might seem cruel. Soon after my arrival, a middle-aged woman, one of the oldest members of the community, related how she had been liberated from her sense of bodily shame by the guru. While she had apparently recovered from the experience, which had taken place several months earlier, it definitely seemed more traumatic than therapeutic to me. On one of the first nights when Da Free John was allowing his followers to drink alcohol, smoke, and dance,[30] Da decided that this overweight, insecure woman was too uptight about her body. As her guru, he ordered her to strip. As a devotee she could either defy her guru and leave the community or take off her clothes. She obeyed the guru and then spent the next half hour dancing naked to acid rock music on top of a table, watched and cheered by the entire community. Was this an example of skillful, compassionate teaching, an exploitative act of sadistic voyeurism, or something else entirely? I honestly do not know, though I am certainly glad I did not have to witness the incident and even happier that I was not placed in her situation.[31]

Another troublesome point concerns Da Free John's sources of legitimacy. On the one hand, he claimed that his insight was unique; others in the past had shared his profound understanding, but no living gurus and masters had reached his level of realization. Therefore no one now living could judge, evaluate, or criticize his radical insights and actions. In his formal talks Da Free John would often discuss various famous teachers and explain where their evolution had stopped. (Almost every potential competitor had become trapped by yogic experiences of bliss, thereby falling short and failing to realize the prior enlightenment beyond all changing, temporary yogic illuminations.) Yet Da Free John had also been the student of several powerful practitioners of shaktipat yoga[32] and spoke freely and fondly of his relationship with these teachers.

Swami Rudrananda (usually simply called Rudi), an American yogi who had studied the Gurdjieff work, practiced Subud, and spent time in Ganeshpuri with Swami Muktananda and Muktananda's guru, Nityananda, still commanded Da Free John's admiration, even though the two had broken contact before Rudi's recent death. Da Free John especially admired Rudi's wild energy and lust for experience. In a sentimental mood, Da Free John once mused, "Rudi loved men, and I love women. Together we could have fucked the world."

Da Free John's relationship with Swami Muktananda is more problematic. A close reading of Da Free John's autobiography, *The Knee of Listening*, suggests that Da Free John fully expected his final teacher, Swami Muktananda, to endorse Da's enlightenment and role as guru.[33] When this did not ensue, the two began a feud that was in full swing when Muktananda visited the Bay area in 1974. Da Free John claimed to have a letter, written in Hindi, that confirmed him as a successor to Muktananda. Whether this is true or not, it reveals clearly that Da Free John felt the need to have his spiritual qualifications confirmed by a recognized authority and suggests that his claims to be beyond the evaluation of others were at least partly defensive in origin. In his evening talks, Da Free John frequently referred to Muktananda as a "black magician." Muktananda spoke of his former student in similar terms.[34] During our weekdays in San Francisco, several of us clandestinely visited Muktananda at his ashram in Oakland. His "presence" was quite similar to Da Free John's, if not more powerful; when he entered a room behind your back, you would involuntarily swivel to see him, as if alerted by a tingling sixth sense; yet his lectures lacked the depth and comprehensive understanding we saw in our guru's.

Towards the end of my stay I began to realize that Da Free John was gradually asserting a claim to be an avatar, an incarnation of God on earth. He actually sets it out in his first book, *The Knee of Listening,* when he describes his childhood experience of basking in "the Bright," his childhood term for the divine light that he experienced from birth.[35] The claim is not that all children are naturally enlightened before they are socialized into our deadened daily awareness; the claim is that little Franklin Jones was uniquely enlightened from birth and is, in fact, God in human form. An avatar does not need the imprimatur of a mere swami or a western yogi.

While establishing his status as an avatar, Da Free John claimed to produce a number of miracles. Most of these "miracles" slipped right by me, unnoticed, but one in particular was especially baffling; since it may have led to my expulsion, I will explain it as best I can.

One Saturday, after an exuberant night of partying and laughter, we passed the day in some sort of celebration, at least I do not remember doing my usual work. The entire community enjoyed the well-earned break, wandering around outdoors, talking and lolling about. Several days later, the community was buzzing with increasingly dramatic tales of the astronomical marvels Da Free John had wrought on that lazy afternoon. Apparently, among other things, the guru had caused the sun to be ringed by a bright purple corona that had been clearly visible for many hours.[36] Devotees vied to describe the miracle in increasingly dramatic terms. Now here is where things get truly puzzling.

I had been outdoors all that afternoon. Not only had I seen nothing out of the ordinary, but no one within my hearing had mentioned anything at all about the miracle at the very time it was supposedly happening! I was not trying to be difficult or obtuse, but this proved too much for me. If a great miracle had occurred, why was it not mentioned at the time? I asked a number of devotees what they had seen and why they had not called everyone's attention to it, but received no satisfactory answers. It slowly emerged that I was not alone in missing this miracle; my skeptical cohorts on the community's fringe were similarly in the dark.

Within several days, we were drawn aside, individually, for somber meetings with the ashram authorities in which we were told that it had been a mistake to accept us into the community without testing; we were welcome to remain as probationary members of the Dawn Horse Communion, but it was unclear when, if ever, we would merit another visit to Persimmon. Several of the skeptics blamed themselves for their lack of spirituality and accepted their punishment. My Canadian roommate and I said farewell to the West Coast and were soon sharing a delirious thirty-hour nonstop drive across the U.S. with two Native Americans we had met through a Haight-Ashbury ride-board. This was the end of my brief involvement with Da Free John, though I kept up with his writings until his word use and capitalization became intolerably idiosyncratic.[37]

CONCLUSIONS

There will be no great summing up of my experiences; the pieces cannot be made to fall neatly into place. To be honest, I do not really have any conclusions, in a scholarly sense, to offer. Rather I would like to present several hypotheses that have helped me get some grip on an otherwise baffling and elusive man whose words and actions I find too fascinating to ignore.

In retrospect, the "miracles" and, most importantly, individuals' reactions to them may provide a key to interpreting the group consciousness that Da Free John was constructing in his community. It seems most likely that no one actually saw the marvels the guru claimed to have produced, but the erstwhile devotees' responses to Da Free John's claims provided a litmus test to determine who had or had not fully surrendered to the guru's version of reality, thereby giving a reliable criterion for weeding the ranks of the rapidly growing community. One is reminded, of course, of the story "The Emperor's New Clothes," with the significant twist that the bratty kid who notices that the Emperor is naked gets punished, and the compliant, self-deceiving officials are rewarded. The motive for purging the community at that particular time seems clear; the following weekend an independent film crew was scheduled to visit Persimmon to film Da Free John and his ashram.[38] It must have seemed imperative to remove all potential dissidents from the set.[39]

Although Da Free John was vociferous in condemning "cultic" behaviors and blamed his ashram members for repeatedly falling into the trap of blind guru worship, the entire organization of the community was designed to inculcate and enforce the very behaviors the guru ostensibly despised. Our "spiritual journals" provided an efficient means for monitoring individuals' attitudes and spotting ideological or behavioral deviations as soon as they arose, in addition to their previously discussed value as tools of self-imposed indoctrination. While it is possible that a controlling, totalistic ideology, with an accompanying "brain police," is almost certain to develop at some point in the life of any tight, committed religious community, it is my opinion that Da Free John was fully conscious of the intense, self-regulating socialization taking place in his community and was most likely the principal author of the systems of control. It seems that there were few areas in the management of the ashram that fell outside the guru's scrutiny. No matter what he said about the spiritual pitfalls of the "cultic mentality," Da Free John insisted upon a community that embraced the most slavish and unquestioning traditions of Indian guru worship.[40]

Any discussion of "cults" or new religious movements soon turns to the titillating topic of "brainwashing." Enquiring minds everywhere love stories of mysterious Rasputin-like gurus whose dark, hypnotic eyes can reduce big-men-on- campus into mindless zombies who annoy people at airports and turn Sunday school-teaching valedictorians into groveling sex slaves. Even the currently respectable Jesus once commanded a group of fishermen to "cast down your nets and follow me"–and they did it.[41] This is pretty exciting stuff, and we can understand why the popular press exploits a topic that excites such strong reader response. Unfortunately, the reality is often more prosaic.

First off, we should consider the term most often used to describe the process of conversion to non-mainstream religious beliefs. "Brainwashing" is not a descriptive term for a recognized, systematic process that can be performed on demand; it is a metaphor.[42] Even those scholars who believe that individuals can be transformed against their will through coercive mind control concede that physical isolation is a necessary part of the process; without imprisonment it cannot be done.[43] In California, Da Free John could not imprison anyone; rather than holding individuals against their will, he made them plead for admission.[44] Given the constant scrutiny directed upon new members, it is fair to suggest that we were intensively socialized, but the pressure to conform came from within at least as much as without. The guru claimed to offer access to profoundly ecstatic spiritual realization, and the only way to gain access to that experience was by playing his game. The better you played the game, by showing your devotion and obedience, the greater your contact with the guru and the more frequent your opportunities for grace. We were all willing, ardent competitors in this game, though some of us came to resent the rules. In the case of new religious movements that use deception and high-pressure manipulation in recruiting, we may be observing a different process, but the Dawn Horse Communion was always clear about what was required to remain in good standing. The Dawn Horse Communion was, and probably still is, far more interested in the commitment of its members than the size of its following.[45] In fact, so far as I know, the community has never gone in for active recruiting, preferring to let people be drawn by Da Free John's writings.

The other "techniques of manipulation" to which new and prospective members were subjected were really quite mild. The restricted vegetarian diet and accompanying fasting can hardly overpower anyone who has a will to begin with, as witnessed by the hundreds of millions of vegetarians worldwide who appear to have control over their decision making. Similar arguments can be made for the practice of daily meditation on the guru's picture. Obviously, the community had an absolute focus on the person of Da Free John, and he figured in nearly every conversation; members became saturated with an atmosphere of devotion and idol-worship, but there was little more coercion in this than one would find among a group of Elvis worshippers on a charter bus pilgrimage to Graceland. The bottom line is that I feel that most of the socialization I experienced was the product of my own will and desires; Da Free John was a splendid salesman, to be sure, convincing hundreds of us that he was the only true master of our time and the only route to liberation, but we coaxed, enticed, and cajoled ourselves and each other into accepting his claims. We are responsible for that choice; no irresistible outside force ran off with our intellects.[46] However, the guru also bears responsibility for his skillful, well-orchestrated processes of manipulation, especially since he presumably knows what his real motives and purposes are. I still do not.

The portrait that emerges from the *San Francisco Chronicle* articles is disturbing and plausible. Da Free John appears to have become a reclusive, binge-drinking misogynist, still brilliant and charismatic, but violent and sadistic towards his most committed and dependent followers. That one of the two men closest to him in 1974 was, in 1985, contemplating a lawsuit for "seventeen years of emotional stress" does not bode well.[47] At the very least, it suggests that Da Free John is an ineffective teacher, since seventeen years of discipleship ought to be long enough for a follower to achieve some of the positive results of meditation, like stress reduction. It is even more alarming to realize that the guru's closest long-term followers felt that they had been manipulated and abused. After all, these are the persons who have been most intimately involved in Da Free John's work of transformation over the course of several decades. If in this time they have not benefited spiritually, could anyone else have?

Yet there is the problem of Da Free John's teachings: they are almost flawlessly constructed, seemingly too brilliant to be the product of an egotistical sociopath. And although most post-modern thinkers must suspect that extraordinary verbal skills are not necessarily associated with spiritual insight and responsible behavior, this gives one pause.

Furthermore, I still cannot dismiss Da Free John's aura of absolute certainty. What is the source of Da Free John's powerful insights and personal confidence, if not an experience of "enlightenment"? Is it indeed possible that Da Free John is what he claims to be: a "fully enlightened" adept? (Leaving aside for the moment what this might possibly mean.) If we provisionally assume that this is true, what are the implications? One would be that an "enlightened being" is not particularly benign. Enlightened sages are not necessarily kind, compassionate, altruistic, courteous, concerned, environmentally aware, politically correct, or any of the wonderful things their publicists proclaim them to be. They are definitely not saints. Would the world be a better place in any conceivable way if everyone experienced this sort of "enlightenment"? (Probably not.) What positive value does enlightenment hold? (Apparently none other than the bliss enjoyed by the enlightened being.)

This brings us to a main point made by Agehananda Bharati in his polemical book on mystical experience, *The Light at the Center*. Bharati claims that the point of mystical experience is the enjoyment of the experience itself. Though the experience of being "One with the universe" seems pregnant with meaning, in fact, the experience does not necessarily confer any particularly deep insight into ontological questions nor does it transform the ethical, intellectual, academic, interpersonal, or spiritual dimensions of the experiencers' lives, no matter what mystics may subjectively experience, ardently believe, and publicly assert.[48] Enlightenment may be a wonderful experience, it may provide an intense subjective sensation of understanding the meaning and purpose of life, but in the final logical analysis it is simply an overwhelming experience; claims that the experience reveals truth just cannot be proven.[49] Therefore those who imagine that the insights of their mystical experiences are objectively "true" may be deluding themselves.

My best guess is that Da Free John might have had one, or a dozen mystical experiences of being one with the divine. He may even be, as he claims, in a continuous state of "god-intoxication." (*Sahaja samadhi* is his term for this state.) If this is true, it seems unavoidable to conclude that the subjective experience of being one with the divine does not, in and of itself, elevate the ethical level of the mystic's interpersonal relationships; if one is abusive, manipulative, and self-centered before the experience, one may well remain that way during and after it.[50] A person experiencing divine union can be filled with certainty, but this divinely inspired confidence may have few points of contact with daily life, leaving the mystic "divinely deluded." This is my best explanation of how Da Free John can project his atmosphere of absolute knowledge, without being insane or a self-conscious fraud. (I should stress that he was not insane in any obvious clinical sense in 1974, and I do not believe him to be a charlatan, as the term is commonly understood.) Though this hypothesis could be developed further, I have already exceeded the bounds of my expertise.

I will end with the overused, but veracious, platitude that "Power corrupts and absolute power corrupts absolutely." In 1974, Da Free John appeared to be experimenting with his power over his community of devotees. Though he may well have thought that he was leading his following to a state of liberation, he was also removing every potential challenge to his absolute control over the flock. His motives are inscrutable and may never be known, but his behavior is relatively well documented. On the basis of his actions, I suspect that Da Free John has become a grotesque parody of the supremely selfless enlightened being he imagines himself to be. Believing that the liberated being is free from all social rules and religious regulations, he has become a fat, boozy tyrant, abusing his nine "wives" and his inner circle, who interpret Da's every action as a lesson from the divine (as channeled through the guru's human form.) The only individuals who could possibly curb Da Free John's excesses are those who most believe in his divinity, and they blame themselves for their lack of understanding when his behavior seems unreasonable. Ironically, the self-obsession that he has diagnosed as the basic human predicament is reflected in everything he now writes; he has become the Narcissus he so forcefully critiques.

Of course, I might be wrong.

POSTSCRIPT

In the nearly two years since "The Strange Case of Franklin Jones" was written, I have had occasion to reflect on some of the tentative conclusions reached during the week I spent composing the essay. Working rapidly, I had allowed the essay to pour out; it basically wrote itself. Once it was done, I did not spend much time reworking the ad hoc, spontaneous analysis, largely because further pondering did not seem to bring greater clarity to the initial observations. However, recent correspondence, particularly with Dr. Georg Feuerstein and John White, has led to the correction and modification of some of my earlier positions. Now that the essay is being republished, I have decided to take advantage of this opportunity to update the manuscript, by attempting a reappraisal and correction of several of my initial assertions.

There have been a few new developments on the Da-watching front in the last few years, ranging from the predictable (a new name, Adi Da, "the Primal Da"?) to the unlikely (Saniel Bonder, one of the most ardent of the guru's devotees and publicists, has set himself up as an enlightened successor to Da, apparently without the approval of the Master). The community continues to exalt Da as the "World Teacher"; his "Emergence" is now being touted as the greatest event in the history of our galaxy, perhaps even the most spiritually significant occurrence since the Big Bang. In video presentations, the guru rarely speaks–officially this is because he is now devoted to his "blessing work" and presumably is engrossed in radiating enlightened energy throughout the universe–but looks brooding and obese. The guru's lifestyle has put some serious miles on his odometer.

Healthy or not, Da Free John is continuing his ambitious publishing agenda. The current venture is the publication of repackaged, edited, expanded, and sanitized versions of his entire corpus. His first book, *The Knee of Listening*, has grown from an original 271 pages to a mammoth 605-page text. Not only have new prefaces, appreciations and appendices been added, but the descriptions of early phases in the guru's life and spiritual search have been significantly rewritten. One suspects that a serious study of the alterations might reveal a great deal about the ways in which Da is reshaping his image for posterity. Ironically, the altered, revisionist texts are being labeled the "New Standard Editions." In addition to the biblical associations evoked by the name, there are delightful Orwellian overtones, for it is one thing for classicists and biblical scholars to examine the oldest extant texts of the Bible, compare the variant readings, consult the commentaries, and then produce authoritative translations of the foundational texts of Judaism and Christianity, and quite another to issue heavily revised versions of books one recently wrote oneself. It is hard not to get the strong feeling that, even more than before, Da is busily creating his own hagiography and working with dogged energy to establish a teaching and community that will carry on after his death.

While on the topic of editing, I should retract my earlier claim that Da Free John's talks were published as originally given. Georg Feuerstein, writer, yogi, and former editor for the Dawn Horse Press, has informed me that all of Da's talks were edited to some degree before publication. In the early days, the editing was done largely by Nina, Da's wife; in later periods, a group of editors reworked the lectures. The extent of editorial emendation varied greatly from talk to talk. With some, the corrections were limited to the deletion of occasional obscenities and impolitic asides. Other talks were thoroughly restructured and revised. The talks that I heard in person were among the least altered, but then most were published in *Garbage and the Goddess*, a book that has been "recalled" and expunged from the guru's bibliography. Apparently, *Garbage and the Goddess* was the result of a failed experiment in open communication, one soon repudiated. In any case, even the lectures presented in that frank book were not wholly unexpurgated, since especially outrageous remarks were excised. Given the great emphasis most gurus seem to place on controlling their public image, I should have known better.

Recruitment is another issue. Based on my experience, I concluded that Da Free John was not especially interested in dragging new members off the streets or out of the shopping malls. Certainly he was a man with a message and a mission, and both human effort and cash were needed to spread the word, but I saw no big push to convert the masses, unless we consider the movie *A Difficult Man* to be a marketing tool. According to Dr. Feuerstein, this is correct as far as it goes. What the new members did not see was the Master's interest in enlisting the assistance and allegiance of the rich and famous. Though Georg is always discreet in his remarks, he implies that the attempts to recruit highly placed persons of influence were often awkward and clumsy, resulting in embarrassment far more often than success.

For the record, I should note that Georg feels that I was too hard on the "miracles" so prized by the community, though he does not explain what he thinks actually took place. His feeling seems to be that devotees desperate for confirmation of their Master's divinity exaggerated the significance of minor synchronisms, atmospheric irregularities, and the like. Rather than making much ado about nothing, as I imply, they were apparently making mountains out of molehills. *Caveat lector*.

In an excellent unpublished paper on Da Free John, the well known author, editor, and consciousness researcher John White makes a simple, obvious point about "service" that struck me with great force. What White notes is that our planet is in desperate straits, largely due to the insensitivity and blundering of human beings. Despite what the "feel good" scientific illiterates of the New Right seem to believe, there is a tremendous amount of work to be done if we are simply going to survive through the next century, much less thrive on a healthy, biologically diverse planet. Even if the earth should prove more resilient than we have any right to expect, there are still vast numbers of vexing social and economic problems that need to be addressed, the sooner the better. What then is the focus of the selfless service promulgated by Da, a man supposedly in profound harmony with the entire spectrum of suffering life forms? The answer is straightforward and simple-minded: all service, from beginning to end, is to be dedicated to satisfying the personal needs of the Guru. Few students of religion would take issue with the necessity, found in any new religious movement, for building an infrastructure and setting up a reasonably permanent and enduring base. All new movements can seem self-absorbed in their initial days. What White objects to is the insistence that Da is essentially the only living being who should be served. Forget the blue whales, the blind Nepalese, and the losers eating out of garbage cans in any American city, serving Da with heart, mind, and soul is the highest, and perhaps the only, good.

Strangely enough, there may be some truth in the Master's claim: devoted service really is liberating. Once again, my worry is with the motives of the guru. Can't the devotees serve Da Free John through serving the needy, much as

Mother Theresa serves Jesus by helping the poor? How do the devotees serving Da differ from those Evangelical Christians who pay lip service to Jesus while doing absolutely nothing to alleviate the suffering of those around them? In fact, the Evangelicals are responsible only for their slanted interpretation of the Christian message, whereas Da, by laying claim to the hearts, souls, and energies of his flock, seems guilty of the most monstrous egotism, unless of course he is truly an avatar, and it turns out that catering to the sexual, financial, and emotional needs of an avatar is of greater cosmic significance than helping the homeless and hungry.

This brings us to the last unanswerable question to be considered in this short piece: What is enlightenment? In my original essay, I entertained the suggestion of Agehananda Bharati that enlightenment, or the "zero experience" as he calls it, is by definition temporary. It cannot be clung to, and anyone experiencing it is basically incapable of normal functioning, for as long as it lasts. Doesn't this go against nearly everything "enlightened" masters have claimed? Not exactly, at least not as Bharati explains it.

Bharati's most effective argument hinges on the distinction between emic and etic modes of speech. Though the nuances of these technical terms drawn from anthropology are not always clear in Bharati's work, basically emic refers to the encoded private language of "in-groups," while etic refers to the language of the "objective" outside observer. Bharati contends that the emic speech of Indian sadhus is governed by complex, unspoken codes, codes that are rarely noticed, much less understood, by outsiders, no matter how clever or perceptive. One of the unwritten rules is that gurus must never acknowledge being in any state other than that of full realization.

"Master, how often do you enter that state of highest bliss and realization?"

"My child, I am in that state even now."

Bharati's claim is that because of the rules governing the speech of Indian mystics, the guru has no choice but to assert that he is always enjoying *satchitananda*, even when he knows perfectly well that he is not. Further, according to Bharati's understanding, the very fact that the guru is exerting himself by speaking in public proves that he is not, in that moment, enjoying the state of enlightenment. If he were, there would be no motive to speak. Most importantly, from the emic perspective of insiders, there is no dishonesty in this claim to permanent enlightenment, despite the undeniable fact that it is objectively false.

Bharati asserts that a dispassionate look at the evidence will suggest, though not prove, that enlightened states are by their very nature temporary. The great mystics are those who frequently enter transcendent states and make the cultivation of the zero experience the dominant focus of their lives, but no one is permanently in the state of highest illumination. The very idea that one can experience enlightenment twenty-four hours a day is the product of a too literal etic understanding of the emic speech of professional mystics, who not incidentally benefit from this linguistic confusion.

If, and this is a very big if, Bharati is right, then one must wonder if the search for ultimate bliss, cosmic closure, and the end to all effort might not be part of the problem, rather than the solution. If all living creatures are engaged in an ongoing process of growth and change, then no one being can ever have all the answers, no one can possibly have reached the end of the path. In traditions where the belief in, and search for, a final realization is a dominant motif, there seem to be marked tendencies towards self-deception, grandiose ego-inflation, and antinomian excess–in short, all the problems that appear to be manifested by Da Free John. My fear is that "permanent enlightenment" is too close to the most private (and selfish?) dreams of most of us to be anything more than a particularly transparent instance of "spiritual" wishful thinking.

Of course, the preceding argument relies heavily on *reductio ad absurdum*. In fact, one cannot assail the logic of a position by pointing to the evil consequences attendant upon acting out its most extreme implications. While it may be true that the spiritual traditions that strive for a final enlightened state, a state that obviates the need for all further work, growth, and morality, tend to produce deluded individuals, this doesn't necessarily give us cause to doubt the existence of the enlightened state. Perhaps a state of "permanent" liberation is, in fact, possible. I don't know.

As I read the New Standard Edition of *The Knee of Listening,* I get the overwhelming impression that Franklin Jones was desperate for some sort of final, ultimate realization, a realization that would provide closure to the search, end the need for any further work, and eliminate the necessity for the struggle and growth that seem to characterize all biological life. Da claims to have reached some sort of supremely enlightened state–despite his own continuing phases of transformation and "emergence," each of which, in turn, has been touted as a final, ultimate, and permanent development. I suspect that Da Free John's insistence on the eternal, unchanging, and incomparable nature of his realization stems more from the personal and all-too-human psychological needs of Franklin Jones than from the uniquely deep illumination of a "World Teacher"; however, even if I am right on this account, it does not prove that Da Free John is not a highly evolved individual. From the time of the Upanishads to the present day, spiritual teachers have warned that the path to liberation is narrow and precarious, with many alluring sidetracks, byways, and dead ends. The farther one progresses, the easier it becomes to fall off the path, which is, by all accounts, "narrow as a razor's edge." Despite Da's many attempts to bolster and augment his "spiritual genealogy," it is clear that his later, most powerful realizations, the ones that have convinced him of his unique status and destiny, have never been publicly confirmed by any other living master. This leads me to suspect that Da may not have transcended his "small self" as completely as he thinks and, having dropped his guard, has slipped off unaware into some kind of high-level ego-trip, albeit one that most of us cannot completely fathom. Nonetheless, it seems likely that Da does, in fact, speak from compelling personal experience, even if the content of his teaching is sometimes questionable. His message now is more clear than ever: despite the fact that we are all one and all equally enlightened in our true nature, we should worship only Da, think only of Da, and serve only Da.

Again, in theory, this devotion should be liberating. Yogi Bhajan once said that if anyone could surrender fully and truly to a rock, they would be liberated. If the way to liberation is through shedding one's limited identification with the mind and body, this may well be true, but then what is the significance of Da and his self-proclaimed exemplary realization? How is an avatar more helpful to a spiritual seeker than a lump of granite?

One answer might be that an avatar, by his or her very presence and example, provides disciples with a living embodiment of full realization, a perfect model for their own transfiguration. Another answer might be that avatars can instruct through personal interactions with disciples, leading each to discover her or his own unique path to Truth. Finally, the avatar might serve as a beacon of enlightened energy, transmuting the gross material of this world into its finer, more spiritual essence. No doubt many other exalted roles can be described for the perfect master. How well does Da fit just these three?

Here I find myself feeling more critical than I did a few years ago. So far as I can tell, Adi Da spends most of his time being worshipped by a handful of especially devoted followers, while he lolls about half-naked in a tropical paradise. This gives the impression that the guru is pursuing a rather oblique approach to enlightening the planet. The video footage of devotees bowing at his feet provides images more appropriately associated with medieval royalty than selfless saints. One can imagine Da in a previous lifetime as a minor European nobleman, exploiting his impoverished serfs, sleeping with their wives and daughters, and living a splendidly dissipated life of luxury, all in the name of the divine right of kings. As a model for proper behavior in the twilight of the twentieth century, Da seems neither better nor worse than, say, Marlon Brando or Keith Richards.

How does Da measure up as a teacher? Who knows? He appears to be at least semi-retired and relying on his books to carry most of his teaching load, having abdicated the role of personal teacher for all but the select few.

The third function of an avatar is less tangible and inherently impossible to measure. Readers will surely rely on their own intuition and experiences to judge the transformative power of any guru, spiritual teacher, or religious leader. This is as it should be. As for me, I've recently begun collecting unusual and distinctive stones; pending the advent of a more plausible "World Teacher," perhaps I'll spend my leisure cultivating my rock garden.

Scott Lowe
19 July 1995
Gousty Knowe

NOTES

1. Franklin Jones is obviously fond of playing with names. For the sake of simplicity I will stick with Da Free John. This is the name under which he seems to have published the most, and I personally find it less obnoxious than some of the others.

2. These articles, by Katy Butler, Rick DelVecchio, and Don Lattin, seem overly sensationalistic and a bit superficial, focusing on sex, drugs, and violence, with little or no attention placed on the community's interpretation of the alleged acts. The documentation is also very weak; all that is reported are the claims of disaffected ex-disciples. (Objective documentation of actions taken on a remote, privately owned, and inaccessible island on the far side of the Pacific is bound to be hard to obtain.) However, I have no doubts that the allegations are essentially true; less extreme but very similar actions have long been a part of the guru's practice.

3. To prepare for writing this essay, I reread the 1985 *San Francisco Chronicle* articles, revived long-dormant memories, and glanced through Da Free John's first three books: *The Knee of Listening*, *The Method of the Siddhas*, and *Garbage and the Goddess*. The first two books had convinced me to visit the community in the first place; the last contains written versions of talks I heard in their original, unexpurgated form while part of the community. For better or worse, I have not consulted other sources on Da Free John or the allegations leveled against him, wishing to avoid additional coloring of my initial impressions and, I hope, non-revisionist memories.

4. For an example of the confusion that results when a guru's follower feigns merely academic interest in his subject, see James Gordon's *The Golden Guru: the Strange Journey of Bhagwan Shree Rajneesh* (Lexington, MA: Stephen Greene Press, 1987). I am not accusing Gordon of any

intentional dishonesty, but it is clear to most readers that Gordon's existential investment in Rajneesh is far greater that he openly acknowledges.

5. It should be obvious that this essay will not be a representative piece of my academic prose. Not only am I exulting in the use (overuse?) of the first person, but I am also striving for a frankness usually censored from scholarly accounts. To counter the discomfort produced by my embarrassing disclosures, I am indulging in a touch of sarcasm and irony from time to time, with the hope that it may prove amusing.

6. The requisite degree of submission varies among the sub-traditions. For example, within Buddhism, only the Tibetans require absolute obedience to the guru's every command; Zen and other Buddhist schools are much less restrictive. However, even the strongest monotheistic religions, Judaism and Islam, have traditions where absolute obedience to the human teacher is the *sine qua non* of spiritual growth.

7. *Matthew* 7:16.

8. This point is obviously debatable, as well.

9. We now arrive at the difficult issue of "crazy wisdom." Proponents of "crazy wisdom" argue that certain great teachers are so profoundly liberated from what they have realized to be arbitrary and meaningless social codes that they are free to act in whatever wild, shocking, or bizarre manner they see fit–all in order to shake their followers out of their deadly complacency, of course. The motive of these masters is compassion, or so we are told; their strange, confusing, amoral, or even apparently hurtful actions are really performed for the ultimate benefit of their disciples, though it may be years before the fruits are harvested. There is a compelling power in the claims made for crazy wisdom; certainly few of us can imagine the long-term

consequences of any actions, and it is wonderful to imagine that supremely liberated individuals can magically act for the ultimate benefit of their followers; however, it is also true that the claims made for "crazy wisdom" are untestable: they can neither be proven nor disproven. The historical records give a glimpse of thousands of ruined lives left in the wake of unscrupulous "spiritual teachers" who used their "divine" status to justify their apparently capricious, damaging whims. (If we stretch the category to include the deluded leaders of messianic movements under the rubric of "crazy wisdom," the toll of ruined lives reaches into the millions. While this might be too broad a use of the term, I believe that a case can be made for classing Hung Hsiu-Ch'uan, the leader of the T'ai-p'ing movement, with other teachers of "crazy wisdom," though he never used the term.) For an introduction to the modern debate, see Georg Feuerstein, *Holy Madness* (New York: Paragon House, 1991).

10. Why is it bad for individuals to kill their neighbors yet glorious for a nation to launch cruise missiles against civilians, to cite a recent instance?

11. I am using the term "members of the community" very imprecisely because, while I was there, the term was not yet clearly defined. A glance through Da Free John's later writings will quickly reveal how hierarchically stratified and legalistically regimented the community has now become. This is not to say that there were not clear demarcations of status, prestige, and privilege; there definitely were, but for the entire period of my association with the community, my personal position was undefined, as was that of several other newcomers. We were certainly not full members, but we were more privileged than the probationary members. I doubt that such ambiguity existed in later periods of the community's life, except of course in the case of beautiful women, who were not required to pass through the initiatory stages required of those less well endowed, a topic to be addressed below.

12. While in San Francisco, my roommate and I supported ourselves by working as bicycle messengers. As one might imagine, the frequent fasts interfered with our work and seemed downright hazardous at the time. When we complained through an intermediary to the guru about the strain we were experiencing from working during the week-long fast, Da Free John reportedly replied that it was an interesting experiment, and he wanted to hear how we fared. My roommate and I were less entertained by the guru's "experiment" and finally broke our fasts on day six, after nearly being killed in separate bicycle-bus collisions. For both of us this appears, in retrospect, to have marked the beginning of the end of our enchantment with the guru.

13. I was told by one of the guru's housekeepers that Da Free John and his "intimate associates" had somehow spent $18,000, in one month, on gourmet food items and booze! If true, this represents almost miraculous excess, given the power of the dollar in 1974.

14. That repetition of a doctrine or belief, even one that one does not accept, leads to gradual attitude change has long been understood in China, where such repetition is a favorite technique of the officials leading "thought reform" campaigns.

15. In retrospect this sycophantic behavior appears nauseating; however, I can happily report that it appeared disgusting at the time, as well. For the newcomers especially, who had far less invested in the community and its belief system, it was relatively easy to keep a level head during those enthusiastic days. Several of us could not refrain from making sarcastic remarks in the face of great acts of "surrender" and self-sacrifice. These remarks may have been a factor in our eventual expulsion.

16. Ramana Maharshi is reported to have done much the same thing for his dying mother (and, somewhat

unorthodoxly, for a pet cow). Since Da Free John was a long-time student of Ramana Maharshi, he was certainly remembering this incident as he ministered to his dying disciple; however, it can always be claimed that Da Free John was simply doing what all true masters do, not copying one of his role models.

Years after this essay was published, I was told that the disciple who fell was seriously injured but not killed. I hope this is true.

17. Generally speaking, in guru-centered communities gossip is the most important means by which ordinary members are educated and socialized in ashram norms. As anyone who has spent time in an ashram will attest, gossip has a paramount role in daily affairs, serving to entertain, uplift, chasten, and motivate the inmates. Who is now closest to the guru? Who is experiencing his *shakti*? Who is sleeping with whom? What did the master really say to X? These and other similarly intriguing questions are answered by gossip networks; securing good access to juicy rumors becomes an important priority for savvy ashramites.

As in other settings, the Dawn Horse Communion had its share of "goody two-shoes" types who eschewed all gossip as spiritually damaging. They were on solid textual ground in this assessment, of course, but the rest of us savored, nay lived for, the gossip that made daily life in the community so exciting.

18. Da Free John seemed to be especially hard on his wife, Nina, often kicking her out of the house, and, if later reports are to be believed, physically abusing her. For the latter see "'Sex Slave' Sues Guru," *San Francisco Chronicle*, 4 April 1985, p. A16.

19. The original *gopis* were the cow-herding maidens of Vrindavan, India, who were so entranced by the youthful

god Krishna that they abandoned their husbands, children, and family responsibilities to adore their lord. In some renditions of the tales of the *gopis,* Krishna multiplies himself into thousands of identical forms so that he can dance with (or alternately make love to) every one of the gopis at the same time. While Da Free John reputedly managed to make love to all the *gopis,* I did not hear that he had ever contrived to manifest more than one bodily form.

20. Da Free John was very convincing in his explanation of the spiritual logic behind these machinations; however, it is hard not to notice that the same destruction of significant human relationships has been used by nearly every "cult" leader since the dawn of record keeping to focus the energies of the followers on the leader, who becomes the sole recipient of his, or very occasionally her, followers' love. Still unresolved, for me, is the question of how, or even whether, interpersonal relationships are to be transcended. Is there spiritual value in traumatically severing human relationships? Is this even the point? Isn't it more likely that negative attachments will fade away on their own as insight deepens? Is the goal to become a heartless, calculating one-man island, unattached to anyone or anything, able to laugh at the suffering and pain of others? In any case, it seems clear that playing with their followers' deepest, most profound relationships has long been one of the favored *modi operandi* of charlatans, frauds, and rascals. For an intriguing parallel see Hugh Milne, *Bhagwan: the God that Failed* (New York: St. Martin's Press, 1986), p. 143 and pp. 149-150.

21. The openness of women to talk of their sexual encounters with the guru led to some extraordinarily embarrassing moments. Without a doubt, the worst of those moments came when a married woman I knew told me, "I'll never forget the first time I went down on the Lord." Even now, nineteen years later, this line makes me wince!

22. I once heard Da Free John claim that Rudi, one of his former teachers, habitually received Swami Muktananda's shaktipat by literally "kissing his ass." While not a practice commonly described in yogic literature, I suppose this could work, if one goes in for such things.

23. Though this astonishingly rapid change in apparent beliefs and values might seem powerful evidence for some sort of sinister "brainwashing" being practiced by Da Free John, I suspect that a simpler explanation will suffice; the compliant young woman was simply overwhelmed by the sudden attention and honor lavished upon her by the guru and his inner circle. In the following weeks, she must have had to undergo the difficult process of restructuring her mental universe to embrace her new experiences.

24. Unfortunately, I do not know the ultimate outcome to this story, though I suspect the ending was unhappy for at least one of the two. When reading the *Chronicle* series, I was hit with an amazed sense of deja vu; an uncannily similar scenario had occurred in 1976, when a Playboy centerfold model and her lover were given similar V.I.P. treatment, with the identical result for the male. Someone in the San Francisco center must have been especially vigilant in satisfying the guru's every need. For the second instance see "'Sex Slave' Sues Guru," *San Francisco Chronicle*, 4 April 1985, p. A1.

25. Da Free John has no monopoly on charisma, of course, but he has, or had, an amazingly powerful personal presence. So did Swami Muktananda and Chairman Mao.

26. I am not a sucker for all gurus, I must hasten to add. For example, the late Rajneesh always impressed me as a fraud of some sort. Though I do not claim to know the level of Rajneesh's spiritual realization, he was a brazen plagiarist who played dangerous games with his *sannyasins'* lives. This was enough to warn me off.

27. Most questions asked in the ashram seemed designed to elicit the guru's approval, or at least his attention, often by showing off the intellectual or spiritual accomplishments of the questioner. Therefore they tended to be fatuous and self-serving.

28. The late Chogyam Trungpa Rimpoche also published impressive "transcripts" of his spontaneous public lectures, but having heard some of these talks in person, I can attest that they have been greatly improved by skillful revision. Rajneesh also expended a great deal of human editorial effort to perfect his "inspired" talks.

29. The ability to make apparent eye contact with a large number of persons simultaneously seems to have been developed by a number of powerful speakers. (Could it be a natural talent?) I once heard a former Hitler Youth leader describe how the Fuehrer appeared to make personal eye contact with him, during a wartime rally attended by over 100,000 young Nazis. He further claimed that everyone at the rally with whom he discussed this reported having the same experience.

30. The arbitrary tightening and relaxing of rules led to great emotional ups and downs; a kind of group hysteria would erupt when, after weeks of rigid asceticism, the guru would declare a party. Within minutes, cases of beer (usually Coors) would appear from somewhere, and everyone would be drinking and smoking "natural" cigarettes. At other times, alcohol, caffeine, and tobacco products were strictly proscribed.

31. An obvious question that no one asked was "what is the relationship between spiritual liberation and freedom from social conditioning?" Does one produce the other? Might they not function entirely independently of one another? Were all the great religious teachers of the past millennia free from shame, guilt, and socially conditioned morality? (I doubt it!) Here is an instance where the guru defined the

terms and established the conditions that gave him absolute control over his disciples' lives, yet may have been operating from faulty, unchallenged premises.

32. *Shaktipat yoga* is not a traditional technical term. I am using it to refer to those teachers who seek to impart "enlightened energy" directly to their disciples. In a sense, nearly all Indian spiritual teachers claim to transmit energy to their followers, but for some this is the whole of their method. Da Free John's teachers belong to the latter group.

33. Franklin Jones, *The Knee of Listening* (Los Angeles: Dawn Horse Press, 1972), pp. 122-130.

34. With hindsight, it is tempting to conclude that they were both right.

35. See Jones, *The Knee of Listening*, pp. 9-10.

36. For a photograph, presumably doctored, of the great event, see the back cover of Bubba Free John, *Garbage and the Goddess* (Lower Lake, CA: Dawn Horse Press, 1974).

37. For a good illustration of Da Free John's eccentric and apparently self-absorbed writing style, see Da Free John, *The Dawn Horse Testament* (San Rafael, CA: Dawn Horse Press, 1985). Da Free John's books are now largely unintelligible to the casual reader.

38. The movie shot in the subsequent weeks, *A Difficult Man*, was shown on many college campuses when finished. As I recall, it was filled with scenes of writhing, sobbing devotees and may not have proven an effective recruiting tool. Were it available on video, I would like to see it again.

39. Even without the imminent arrival of the film crew, a showdown was inevitable. Several of the malcontents had defiantly taken to puffing cigarettes behind the dorms (I had been an adamant nonsmoker only weeks before!),

drinking forbidden coffee, and developing our own mocking vocabulary (referring to the *gopis* as "guppies," etc.)

40. Reverence for the guru is an integral part of most Indian spiritual paths; however, the degree of devotion and obedience required by Da Free John, while not outside the range of acceptability in India, places him at an extreme end of the scale.

41. See *Matthew* 4:19.

42. It is also a direct translation from the Chinese. Political cadres in the People's Republic of China are reasonably proficient at inducing behavioral changes in imprisoned subjects through an intensive process of "thought reform." One of the terms they use for this is *xi nao*, which literally means "wash brains." Needless to say, this term is used poetically, not literally.

43. For a persuasive critique of the whole concept of "brainwashing" in new religious movements, see John T. Biermans, *The Odyssey of New Religious Movements: Persecution, Struggle, Legitimation* (Lewiston, N.Y.: The Edwin Mellen Press, 1986), pp. 23-36.

44. The conditions for much more potent manipulation would exist on an isolated private island.

45. In 1985 the Communion claimed a total membership of about 1,100. This is quite small for a group with such a high public profile.

46. Perhaps I was too peripheral to the community to make this claim. Certainly the pressures brought to bear on fully committed members may well have been many orders of magnitude stronger than the still considerable forces I felt. Though I dislike and mistrust the word brainwashing–especially since it is so often trivialized and misused by

both the media and the public–the power of the community and guru to mold and refashion thought should not be underestimated.

47. "Guru's backers say defectors trying extortion," *San Francisco Chronicle*, 7 April 1985, p. B1.

48. Agehananda Bharati, *The Light at the Center* (Santa Barbara, CA: Ross-Erikson, 1982), pp. 87-111 and elsewhere.

49. Please note that I am asserting nothing about mystical experiences other than the obvious fact that thousands of individuals are positive that they have had them and that, logically speaking, the intensity of an experience is no proof of the truth value of its content. Whether there is "really" such a thing as being "One with the divine" is beyond my knowledge and the aims of this article.

50. Bharati not only makes this claim, his own actions provide a living testimonial to its truth! See Bharati, *The Light at the Center*, p. 91.

About the Authors

Scott Lowe is a Professor of Religious Studies at the University of Wisconsin. He has a Ph.D. in the History of Asian Religions from the University of Iowa and teaches courses in "Introduction to World Religions", "Sacred Earth: Religion and Nature" and "Asian Religions in the West". He has traveled extensively in China, Taiwan, Mexico, Turkey, and Europe and speaks and reads Mandarin Chinese.

David Lane is a Professor of Philosophy at Mt. San Antonio College. He is also a Lecturer in Religious Studies at California State University, Long Beach. He received his Ph.D. in the Sociology of Knowledge from the University of California, San Diego, where he was also a recipient of a Regents Fellowship. Widely traveled he has authored numerous books, including *The Radhasoami Tradition* and *The Making of a Spiritual Movement*.

35300444R00060

Made in the USA
Middletown, DE
27 September 2016